and Fred ask Hobson for a thousand pounds, but Maggie says that Hobson can only afford five hundred pounds, which is agreed upon. It is revealed to Hobson that Alice and Vickey are going to marry Albert and Freddie.

A year later business is very slow in Hobson's shop as there is no work coming in – the trade has gone to Willie and Maggie. Hobson is hopelessly depressed and hinting at thoughts of suicide. A doctor comes to look at Hobson and quickly diagnoses chronic alcoholism. He says that Hobson needs someone to keep an eye on him. At this point Maggie arrives, and she says that she must ask Willie whether they can move back in with Hobson. Alice and then Vickey arrive and make it clear that they will not move back to the shop (Vickey is expecting a child). Willie arrives, and Alice and Vickey learn that he cannot be bossed around any more – he asks them to leave. Willie tells Hobson that he will only come back if he and Hobson are partners in the business, but with Hobson a sleeping partner with no influence, and the shop will be called Mossop and Hobson. Willie is now in charge.

■ Contents

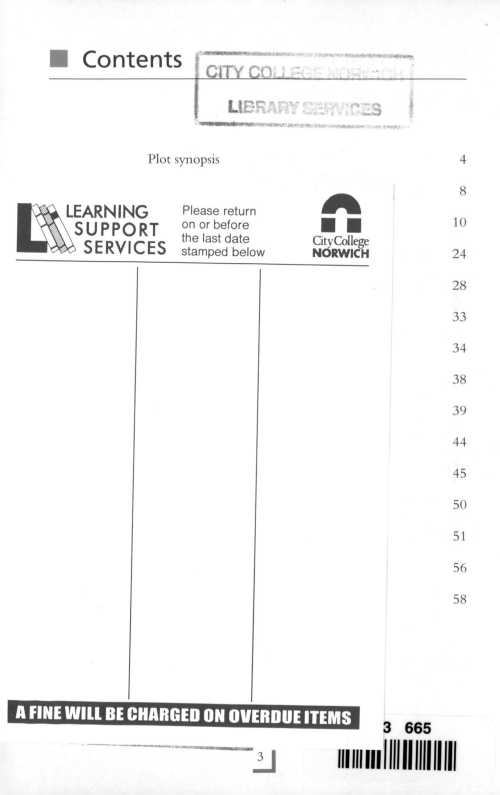

■ Plot synopsis

The play takes place in Salford, near Manchester, in 1880. Harold Hobson is a widower who owns a shoe shop, where his three unmarried daughters work. His daughters have lately become too 'bumptious' for his liking, and he decides that he should marry off Alice and Vickey, the two youngest, but he soon changes his mind when his friend Jim Heeler says that he will have to pay for 'settlements'. He does not even consider marrying off Maggie, his eldest daughter, as he thinks that at thirty she is already on the shelf, and in any case she is a good worker. Maggie has other ideas however. Mrs Hepworth, a highly respected customer, comes in to find out who made her shoes, because she is very pleased with them. Willie Mossop, one of the shoemakers that Maggie has had her eye on, made them. This convinces Maggie that she must marry Willie as she is such a good saleswoman and he is such a good cobbler. When Maggie is in the shop on her own she calls Will in and proposes to him. He is very taken aback and initially resists, claiming that he doesn't love Maggie, and that he is already engaged to someone else. However, Maggie will not accept no for an answer, and Will finally agrees to the idea. Alice, Vickey and Hobson are all very disapproving of the match, but Maggie says that if Hobson doesn't accept the situation and agree to start paying her a wage, she and Willie will leave and set up in business on their own.

A month later we find that business is slow at Hobson's shoe shop, and that Maggie and Willie have set up in business together and are about to be married. They call at the shop to invite Vickey, Alice and their respective suitors Fred Beenstock and Albert Prosser to the wedding. Maggie has a plan to enable her sisters to marry the men they have chosen. A drunken Hobson has fallen into the cellar of Beenstock's grain warehouse, and Albert has drawn up a writ for trespass against Hobson. Freddie deposits this on top of the sleeping Hobson and then joins the others at the wedding.

After the wedding they go back to the cellars for the wedding breakfast. As the guests are preparing to leave Hobson arrives. Alice, Vickey, Albert and Freddie are sent into the bedroom while Maggie and Willie speak to Hobson. He has come because he is in trouble and he wants to discuss with Maggie the action for damages for trespass. Maggie says that what he is most afraid of is appearing in court, so therefore he must attempt to settle things out of court. Maggie then calls Albert (as the lawyer) and Fred out of the bedroom. Albert

'He's snoring very loudly, but he isn't hurt. He fell soft on some bags.'

A Lancashire comedy

Maggie Do you call this English?
Albert Legal English, Miss Hobson.
Maggie I thought it weren't the sort we talk in Lancashire.

Hobson's Choice is a play which not only belongs very firmly in its period, but also in its place, and that place is Salford, Lancashire. We can find a number of examples of references, words and particular ways of speaking to illustrate this. Maggie and Albert exchange the lines above when Albert brings her the writ after Hobson has fallen into the cellar. At another point Hobson says, 'if you mean to be a factor in the world in Lancashire...'. Maggie sums up the attitude of her father with the words 'It's news to me we're snobs in Salford.'

The most obvious references to something which was very typical of working-class life in Lancashire in the nineteenth century are the references to clogs. A Lancashire clog had a leather upper but a wooden sole and was worn by many of the mill workers. One of the reasons why Tubby could go on making clogs when there were no orders was that clogs would always sell and there was no harm in stockpiling a number of pairs. They were also very cheap and there was no real profit to be made out of them. Life in Salford was generally very poor. The person in the play who wears clogs is Ada Figgins and, at one point, Maggie talks about selling her a pair. Maggie sums up the way of life: 'A Salford life's too near the bone to lose things through fear of speaking out.'

The place of women in this society was very particular. Hobson makes it clear that the man is in charge of the family (or so he would like to think), as was the convention of the day, but Jim Heeler says that, when they step out of line, it is his wife who leathers his daughters, showing a very physical attitude to discipline; it is Ada's mother who will give Willie a thick ear to bring him back into line.

We should look at some of the words and phrases which put the play in its place:

'you'll none rule me'	You'll not tell me what to do
'I should do nowt of kind'	I shall do nothing of the sort
'I'm fair moithered'	I'm all confused/mixed up
'tokened'	engaged/betrothed
'I'll give you best'	I'll give in to you/acknowledge you're in charge

'She'll jaw me till I'm black in the face'	She'll keep telling me off until I collapse
'gradely lot of brass'	a considerable amount of money
'nobbut'	only
'howst feeling'	how do you feel
'gaffer'	the boss
'his temper so nowty and all'	his temper is so short/changeable
'You'll not do owt of sort'	You'll do nothing of the kind
'You're not a toper'	You're not a heavy drinker

When discussing the language of the play we should also consider the one character who is more of a caricature, Dr Macfarlane. He is Scottish and what he says is virtually a parody of what we expect the Scottish doctor to say: 'Do ye ken that ye're defying me? Ye'll die fighting will ye?'

Maggie and Willie sum up the geographical feel of the play in the simplest of ways when they look at each other at the end of the play and say:

> **Maggie** Eh lad!
> **Willie** Eh lass!

Who's who in *Hobson's Choice*

Henry Horatio Hobson

It would be easy for Henry Hobson to be portrayed as a very unsympathetic character: he is a bully; he is thoughtless; he is selfish; he is mean; he is cruel. It is important though, for the play as a whole, that we are able to feel sympathy for him, as this gives him the added dimensions which enable us to see him as a fully rounded character. He is naive; he is at times unsure of himself; he doesn't know how to cope with problems; he ultimately suffers from depression and melancholy; he cannot control his drinking.

Hobson is a widower and, although we know little about his wife, she is mentioned once by him when he is talking to Jim Heeler:

'Ah, Jim, a wife's a handy thing, and you don't know it proper till she's taken from you. I felt grateful for the quiet when my Mary fell on rest, but I can see my mistake now.'

She had some control over Hobson and, more importantly, she had some control over their daughters, which Hobson does not have. Perhaps, in some ways, she was like Maggie.

There is ample evidence to show Hobson as a bully, most notably when he believes he can solve everything by beating Willie with his leather belt. He believes in physical violence as a form of discipline, and it is clear that he would happily have his daughters subjected to a similar form of punishment if his wife was there to administer it.

His thoughtlessness is illustrated at the beginning of Act Two, when Alice is at a loss as to what Tubby should do. It is Hobson's shop, and he should be there to manage it, especially after the departure of Maggie, but he is not there to give the orders to the workroom. His treatment of Tubby later in the play, when Tubby has prepared his breakfast, is equally thoughtless: 'Then go and look. And take that bacon with you. I don't like the smell.'

Hobson spends his life going out to the pub and drinking to excess with his friends, which is probably the best example of his selfishness. He does not consider that Maggie spends all her time in the shop in his absence. He is not concerned about the time he gets home for a meal, and tries to exert his selfish authority. He pays his daughters no wages and underpays his workmen: 'Wages? Do you think I pay wages to my own daughters? I'm not a fool.' His meanness is tied up at some points with his lack of business acumen. He cannot cope when, towards the end of the play, Willie talks of re-designing the shop. He cannot see that, by investing and improving things, he will in fact improve his takings and therefore his profits. All he sees is that spending money should be avoided. It is ironic that, when Willie and Maggie return, his business is only worth about £200 in Willie's estimation.

There are a number of examples to show that Hobson is not the man of the world that he thinks himself, and that in fact he is very naive. It doesn't occur to him that he has a responsibility towards his daughters' weddings, and when Jim refers to the necessity of a financial settlement, a typically unreasonable response is produced.

He is very unsure of himself when Mrs Hepworth arrives at the shop, and as a result he behaves rather stupidly. He is very frightened of failure and he believes she has come to complain. His uncertainty means that Mrs Hepworth turns to Maggie, believing that she will get more sense out of her. The lack of sureness is also seen very clearly in the last Act when Hobson subordinates himself to Tubby and agrees with Tubby's suggestion that Maggie be fetched. He is also, at that time, unable to cope with the doctor. He fools himself as long as he possibly can and, when he can't cope, he goes into a state of depression, threatening suicide. This cry is in the hope that sympathy will be forthcoming. His attempts to assert authority at this time are futile:

'I've had my liquor for as long as I remember, and I'll have it to the end. If I'm to be beaten by beer I'll die fighting, and I'm none practising unnatural teetotalism for the sake of lengthening out my unalcoholic days. Life's got to be worth living before I'll live it.'

In some ways you could say that the play is about the humiliation of Hobson. As Willie and Maggie go up in the world, Hobson has to go down. Willie has to be forceful in their last encounter to show his own new found strength. The sadness of Hobson's situation is perfectly illustrated by the offer he makes to Willie and Maggie when he makes his final attempt to keep in control: 'and if that's not handsome, I dunno what is.' He doesn't!

Maggie Hobson

Maggie can be seen as the driving force in the play; in many ways she controls the destinies of all the other main characters. She is thirty, the eldest of Hobson's daughters, and as far as the rest of her family is concerned she is destined to remain a spinster whose job is to look out for the family, and Hobson in particular. It is obvious that, since the death of her mother, she has been in charge of looking after everything – the shop and the home – and as a result has watched her youth disappear. It is clear that she is in charge of the organisation of mealtimes, controlling the behaviour of her father and sisters. She is an extremely good salesperson: Willie may have made Mrs Hepworth's shoes, but Maggie sold them to her; she always has an eye to a potential customer and is perfectly prepared to exploit a situation, as she does when Albert is in the shop and ends up buying a new pair of boots, much against his will. She is even prepared to try and sell Ada Figgins a pair of clogs, having just taken Willie from her.

Initially we must feel a great sympathy for Maggie because of the way in which she is treated. For instance, when Hobson is telling Alice and Vickey they will get married, Maggie asks, 'If you're dealing husbands round, don't I get one?', and gets the reply: 'Well, that's a good one! … You with a husband! … you're past the marrying age. You're a proper old maid, Maggie, if ever there was one.' Maggie is not appreciated by her family, although she is appreciated by Mrs Hepworth in her rather abrupt way: 'Young woman, you seemed to have some sense when you served me. Can you answer me?'

On some occasions we might feel considerable sympathy for others who come within her orbit: Albert, who has no control over his purchase of boots; her sisters, who do as they are told; Willie, who appears to have no control over his destiny – 'When I make arrangements, my lad, they're not made for upsetting.'

Yet it is not just a case of being domineering. Maggie certainly knows what she wants, but she starts from a belief that she really does know what is best for others, and there is a considerable amount of generosity in her make-up. For example, when you analyse the whole episode of Hobson falling down the cellar it is to find that the financial motive is simply to provide her sisters with a settlement for their marriages. Maggie had no settlement when she married Willie, and she never considered herself in the arrangement. She wants her sisters to be happy and will do her utmost to make sure that they are.

Where Willie is concerned, Maggie is frequently insistent on taking a back seat to him; she is not out to dominate him. Ironically, we are made to feel that if he had remained with Ada he would have been dominated and would never have got anywhere. Ada's mother would have been in complete control and Willie would just have done as he was told. By contrast Maggie wants to help Willie develop; she sees a potential in him which perhaps no-one else sees. As Willie says in bewilderment at the beginning of their relationship, 'I'm your best chance?'. Maggie spends the rest of the play helping Willie develop that potential, through education and encouragement – 'Now you've heard what I've said of you tonight. In twenty years you're going to be thought more of than either of your brothers-in-law.'

At the end of the play Maggie will not make any decision about coming back to live with Hobson; it will be Willie's decision and she will defer to him. It is quite clear that if Willie had said that they were to go back to the cellar she would have gone with him. She only makes one slight intervention in the situation and that is when she tries to argue about the name of the shop, but her influence is gentle: 'Don't spoil it, Will … You're the man I've made you and I'm proud.' Willie's reply is a comment on their relationship: 'Thy pride is not in the same street, lass, with the pride I have in you.'

It is important to remember that Maggie is a very loving person, and we do see the moment of sentimentality when she saves one of the flowers from her bouquet to press in her bible, but perhaps the background against which she has been brought up doesn't allow her to show that love until she is very sure both of herself and others. She is proud, fiercely proud of the things which she has a right to be proud of: her business ability, her husband. She is also very humble and has very clear values. When she is married Willie puts a brass ring on her finger which she has bought out of the shop's stock for a few pence. When Willie wants to remove it and replace it with a gold one at the end of the play the humility and generosity in her character shines through:

> 'What are you doing? You leave my wedding ring alone.'
>
> 'You've worn a brass one long enough.'
>
> 'I'll wear this ring forever, Will.'
>
> 'I was for getting you a proper one, Maggie.'
>
> 'I'm not preventing you. I'll wear your gold for show, but that brass stays where you put it, Will, and if we get too rich and proud we'll just sit down together quiet and take a long look at it, so as we'll not forget the truth about ourselves …'

Maggie is the realist who will always remember.

William Mossop

Central to the play is the development of Willie Mossop from a worker in Hobson's business to a successful businessman in his own right. It cannot be said that it is all down to Maggie. Right from the start, from the entrance of Mrs Hepworth, it is clear that Willie has an exceptional talent for making boots and shoes. The potential is there and it only needs someone to unlock that potential for Willie to blossom. Initially the majority would be willing to write Willie off simply because of his background which gave him very little chance. We are reminded of the social and historical background of the time when Hobson says: 'You can't have Willie Mossop. Why, lass, his father was a workhouse brat. A come-by-chance.' Willie should therefore be satisfied with what he has got. That is not only the opinion of Hobson and his two younger daughters, it is also the view of Ada and Mrs Figgins. Two people are prepared to look beyond that with Willie.

Maggie has not reached a sudden decision when she makes the proposal to Willie that they should join forces;

she has been thinking about the possibility for six months. Willie does not fight the proposal in one sense – he sees that their combined talents could make a partnership – what he is not prepared for is that the partnership will also be a marriage. If he tries to fight that aspect of the situation it is because one of Willie's qualities is an immense loyalty to his present situation. He does not see himself leaving the shop, partly because of the security it provides, but also because he is very loyal in the same way as Tubby is. If he protests that he cannot marry Maggie it is also out of his loyalty to Ada. If the battle is between Maggie and Ada for him, he will go along with the result partly out of fear, but partly because he owes a loyalty to both of them and cannot make a decision. What is clear is that he is happy with the outcome: 'It's like an 'appy dream. Eh, Maggie, you do manage things.'

The other person who can see Willie's potential is Mrs Hepworth. She publicises Willie's ability and is ready to show her faith in him by making a loan to get him started. There is no doubt that her confidence in him helps not only in the practical way of providing him with his first customers, but also in boosting his confidence. We quickly find out that Willie has the aptitude to learn and is keen to do so. Maggie says that his writing is improving fast.

It is important for us to be able to believe that the transformation of Willie in Act Four is a real possibility – from the moment he enters he is in control: 'Now, then, Maggie, go and bring your father down and be sharp. I'm busy at my shop, so what they are at his.' When Alice tries to tell him that he will do 'what's arranged for you' she is perhaps a little surprised at the reply: 'I'll do the arranging, Alice. If we come here, we come here on my terms.' His greeting of Hobson is very much to the point: 'Aye. Don't let us be too long about this. You've kept me waiting now a good while and my time's valuable. I'm busy at my shop.' He remains in control of the situation throughout the final part of the play, although he surprises himself by it: 'Words came from my mouth that made me jump at my own boldness...' It is summed up in the final stage direction and in the last words of the play:

'Will comes down with amazement, triumph and incredulity written on his face, and attempts to express the

inexpressible by saying –

"Well, by gum!" '

By the end of the play the audience believes that Willie has the ability to go on succeeding. He has the vision, as is shown in the comments he makes about the look of the shop, the carpet and the leather-covered chairs. He may well reach St Anne's Square.

Alice Hobson

Alice and Albert

We are told very little about Alice in the opening stage direction. She is the middle of Hobson's three daughters and is twenty-three. She is wearing a black apron and she is knitting. Perhaps it is significant that Vickey is described as being pretty, whereas Alice is not. She is being courted by Albert Prosser who visits her in the shop, but she is unable to tell her father about the relationship. She is less forthright than Vickey when they are talking with their father of the clothes they wear. What is important to Alice is that she is fashionable: 'It is not immodest, father. It's the fashion to wear bustles', 'We shall continue to dress fashionably, father.'

Alice is very much against Maggie marrying Willie, but mainly because she thinks Albert will feel he will not be able to associate with the family. After Maggie and Willie have gone she tries to assume Maggie's role, but is not capable of doing so. When she is forced into a decision and sends Tubby to make clogs it is not really her decision at all, it is Tubby's. She gets so desperate with herself that she can't even add up. On the day of the wedding she is almost relieved to allow Maggie to take over again, and asks her to help with the books, which Maggie refuses to do. Whatever the situation Alice still sees herself as superior through her association with Albert, even if she is unable to develop the situation herself.

Towards the end of the play, when she is married to Albert, we see Alice's snobbery quite clearly: 'Ah, well, a fashionable solicitor's wife doesn't rise so early as the wife of a working cobbler.' Her reply to the possibility of coming to live with her father is simply, 'I live in the Crescent myself', and she makes it quite clear that she will certainly not be coming. It would not be true to say that Alice is unpleasant, but she is lacking in intelligence. It is, at the last, absolutely clear that she doesn't understand that any wealth Hobson may have had was tied up in the shop and, when Willie tells her the truth, that her father is worth very little, she can only ask, 'Do you man to tell me father isn't rich?'. At the end she may sweep to her gloves on the table, but it is right that she is sent packing.

Vickey Hobson

Vickey is introduced as being twenty-one and very pretty, the youngest of Hobson's three daughters. At the opening of the play she is reading. She is very lively and believes that she can twist her father round her little finger. She is also selfish. Her father says of her, 'Vickey, you're pretty, but you can lie like a gamester' when they are talking about new dresses, and he gets what might be considered a petulant or a very rude reply: 'We shall dress as we like, father, and you can save your breath.' Vickey is a snob, but rather less so than Alice, perhaps because in her naive way she doesn't see the implications which Alice sees in things.

At the beginning of Act Two Vickey is still reading and is no help whatsoever in helping sort out what Tubby ought to do. At the beginning of Act Two she also reveals her affection for Fred Beenstock. Perhaps we are led to feel that there is a genuineness in her relationship with Fred, and perhaps at the end she has a rather more genuine reason for being unable to look after Hobson as she is pregnant with her first child at the time.

The best way to describe Vickey is 'flighty'. One minute she is displaying a great deal of affection; the next minute she is finding fault and being unpleasantly vicious.

'Oh, do stop talking about your husband. If Alice and I don't need to ask our husbands, I'm sure you never need ask yours. Willie Mossop hasn't the spirit of a louse and we know it as well as you do.'

One minute she is following Alice's snobbery; the next minute she is displaying a glimmer of Maggie's common sense: 'You know, mended up, those chairs would do very well for my kitchen when I'm wed.' In the end it is her selfishness which wins through, as we see in Act Four when she is not prepared to return to help her father. It is she who takes the initiative with Alice in outlining the danger as she sees it:

'Yes. But we've got to be careful, Alice. She mustn't have things too much her way ... Suppose poor father gets worse and they are here, Maggie and Will, and you and I – out of sight and out of mind. Can't you see what I mean?'

Together with Alice she decides that her father must make his will at once. However unreasonable Hobson may be, he is right when he tells her to leave and go back to her own home.

Albert Prosser

Alice and Albert

Albert was born into a fairly wealthy and privileged family, and nepotism has clearly determined his career. A junior partner in the firm, he will inevitably become a senior partner as he goes on and will lead a very comfortable life. Everything has been handed to him on a plate. Having said that, it seems that Albert is not the strongest of people. When he first comes on the scene he is welcomed by Alice who tells him that her father is still at home. His response to this is to try to make a dash for it. He is clearly scared of Hobson. Neither does he have the strength of character to cope with Maggie, with the result that he buys a new pair of boots when he feels he doesn't need them. It is also clear that, for a considerable time, he has been buying a pair of bootlaces a day from Maggie. He is dominated again by Maggie when he is caused, against his better judgement, to wheel the handcart through the streets with the old furniture on it: 'Yes, but to push a hand-cart through Salford in broad daylight! ... Suppose some of my friends see me?' There is also the matter of the washing up in Act Three.

It is not only Maggie though, who dominates him: Alice also does, as is clear when she forbids him to speak after Willie at the wedding breakfast and he obeys. Perhaps we get the feeling that although he might be professionally successful as a lawyer, at home he will be a rather nagged husband.

Albert has two clear functions in the play. Firstly, Alice needs a suitable partner and he meets that need. Secondly, a lawyer is needed who can be called on to perform several necessary functions, including writing the writ which is to be served on Hobson and the deed of partnership between Willie and Hobson. Albert meets both of these needs.

Fred Beenstock

Freddie is a young successful tradesman, working in the family firm. The first time that we meet him it is revealed that he and Vickey are attracted to each other. He is smart and the sort of person that, on a good day Hobson might actually approve of as a son-in-law. The family firm owns the warehouse into the cellar of which Hobson manages to fall. Freddie does not have the strength himself to deal with Hobson, but he is quite happy to go along with Maggie's idea about the writ. Freddie is quite happy to accept Maggie's help and to do the things that she demands of him. With very little objection he agrees to get his coat off and to help Willie get the sofa down the stairs, and he takes the writ to put on Hobson on his way to the church for the wedding. He tries to make a small objection to doing the washing up, but realises that he and Albert need to keep on the right side of Maggie while she is sorting out the problems which surround his own desire to wed Vickey.

Freddie is clearly a perfectly suitable match for Vickey, and we suspect that they will have a happy marriage. That, then, is his job in the play. He provides an open trapdoor into a cellar, a basis for a writ, a helpful pair of hands at the right time, and himself as a suitable husband.

Mrs Hepworth

Mrs Hepworth only makes one appearance in the play, but she plays a very important role, almost as a guardian angel watching over Willie and Maggie throughout the rest of the play. She is the significant customer arriving in a carriage and living at Hope Hall; Hobson's behaviour on her arrival, grovelling on the floor and fondling her foot makes this very clear. She is precise and clear in what she wants, which is to know the identity of the maker of her boots; she is not satisfied with the answer which would normally be given, that they were the shop's own make, she wants to know exactly who in the workshop made them. Her insistence is such that there is almost an inevitable assumption on the part of Hobson that something is wrong. She gives her card to Willie and insists that, in future, he will make all her shoes and those of her family as well, and will inform her should he move on.

Mrs Hepworth is clearly wealthy and we can either term her generous or acknowledge her to be someone who knows a good investment when she sees one: she loans money to Willie and Maggie to set up their shop and takes her trade, and probably the trade of others to them. She is not a snob and we feel that she doesn't mind that the shop is set up in a cellar. A mark of her generosity is that she has provided Maggie's wedding bouquet from her hot-house. It could almost be argued that she is instrumental in bringing Maggie and Willie together, in that it is after her visit that Maggie knows that her belief in Willie is justified and she moves in to propose marriage to him.

Timothy Wadlow

Tubby, as he is known, is a very important person in the action because he makes decisions, causes things to be done and is always there at key moments. His position in the shop is that of shoehand foreman and, if anyone taught Willie how to make shoes, it was Tubby. His first appearance is very brief and it is simply to provide the information to Mrs Hepworth that Willie made her boots. We then see him in a more significant role at the beginning of Act Two. Tubby knows his place and, although he is perfectly intelligent, it is not his place to make decisions about what should be made in the workshop. He therefore insists on Alice making the decision in the same way as Maggie would have done. In explaining why he needs Alice to make a decision he also provides us the with information about what has been going on; all the high-class trade has been disappearing and the only thing which can be made without orders being placed are clogs which can be stock-piled, although Tubby tells us that there is very little profit in them.

Early in the play he provides Willie with a bed, and also goes and collects his things from the Figgins' so that Willie does not have to face Mrs Figgins. He takes charge of the shop while the others go off to celebrate the wedding.

In many ways it would have seemed sensible for Tubby to leave and find another position, but he is immensely loyal to Hobson, and he is still there at the beginning of Act Four: 'I'm an old servant of the master's, and I'm sticking to him now when everybody's calling me a doting fool because I don't look after Tubby Wadlow first ...' By the end of the play he has more or less given up performing his real job and is there running errands, fetching the doctor and Jim Heeler, and cooking breakfast for Hobson. He could be bitter, but he is very generous towards both Willie and Maggie and does not blame them for the problems of the shop: 'Willie's a good lad, though I say it that trained him... Miss Maggie, now... well, she's a marvel, aye, a fair knock-out.' Tubby understands the problems of the shop better than Hobson; he knows that, with proper management, the shop could have recovered from Maggie and Willie leaving, but the management has not been good. Perhaps the only bit of initiative Tubby takes is when he suggests that Maggie should be fetched when Hobson is ill. One of his functions may be to show us where Willie would have stayed if Maggie hadn't taken charge.

Jim Heeler

Jim's role is to be there with and for Henry Hobson. He is one of the friends with whom Hobson drinks at the 'Moonraker's'; although others are mentioned, he is the only one who appears. He is described as Hobson's boon companion.

The advantage which Jim has over Hobson is that he has a wife who clearly supports him in the upbringing of their children; his attitude is very much the same as the attitude of Hobson: '... they mostly do as I bid them, and the missus does the leathering if they don't.' His similarity with Hobson is emphasised by the doctor who sees him going the same way as Hobson towards chronic alcoholism. However, there are moments when he shows himself to be rather less naive than Hobson, perhaps notably when they are talking about getting Hobson's daughters married – Jim talks about settlements, which simply produces the naive response in Hobson that he has changed his mind because he is unprepared to spend the money.

Ada Figgins

Ada Figgins is 'tokened' to Willie Mossop at the beginning of the play. It is worth remembering the stage direction which introduces her:

'Ada Figgins enters from the street. She is not ridiculous, but a weak, poor-blooded, poor-spirited girl of twenty, in clogs and shawl …'

She is, of course, the antithesis of Maggie and does not stand a chance against her. She does, however, make a spirited attempt to hang on to the man she wants: 'I see the lad I love, Miss 'Obson.' 'You mind your own business, Miss 'Obson. Will Mossop's no concern of thine.' In the end though, all she can manage is: 'It's daylight robbery.' During this exchange Willie is completely irrelevant and takes no part in the decision making, just waiting to see which one of them will win. In the end it is made clear that it is Ada's mother who is the decision maker, and this is the final admission which Maggie needs to see Ada off.

As is quite common with minor characters in plays, Ada has her job to do, which is to act as a foil for Maggie during the brief moment when the decision about Willie's future is being made and justified. We also see why Maggie is the right person for Willie. Maggie will fill him with ambition for success; Ada would just have hung around his neck allowing him to continue being a bullied and brow-beaten bootmaker, bullied by Hobson and Mrs Figgins, and ultimately by Ada herself.

Dr Macfarlane

Dr Macfarlane appears only in the last act of the play when he is called in to examine Hobson. His diagnosis is immediate and correct (that Hobson is melancholy and depressed due to 'chronic alcoholism'), but he is not prepared to state it while Jim Heeler is there. He is tired from having been up all night at the birth of a baby; he is annoyed that Hobson is well enough to be downstairs; he is bad-tempered and rude, and certainly does not apologise for being so. His understanding of Hobson is clearly expressed in the sentence: 'Your complaint and your character are the same', and is further demonstrated by an instinctive and immediate understanding of what has happened between Hobson and his daughters, hence the prescription of both mixture and Maggie.

In some ways Dr Macfarlane is virtually a caricature, with his written Scottish accent: '… but ma medicine willna do him any good…' There is an importance, however, in the doctor being an outsider rather than being from Salford, and hence looking at Hobson with a very objective eye.

Themes and images in *Hobson's Choice*

Family relationships

Family relationships

The play is about the Hobson family and, as the play develops, about the extended family which will include the three husbands. In many ways the family relationships are very typical of the period, in that Hobson expects to be in charge, and he expects his daughters to look after him and to work for him without question. Certainly, until the time of the action of the play his daughters would have not found this situation in any way a problem, as it is what they would have believed to be an acceptable state of affairs. Maggie has looked after the family and the shop since the death of her mother, and she may have expected to go on doing so if family relationships had not begun to break down.

The relationships begin to break down in a variety of ways. Clearly the death of Mrs Hobson was a sad event of enormous importance, and it leads to the steady decline of Hobson and to his increasing inability to carry out his family role. It puts Maggie in her predicament of running the shop and the family, and perhaps it takes away what might have been a stabilising influence for Alice and Vickey, although this is mere speculation.

The other way in which the family begins to break down is the perfectly natural way that, as the daughters grow up, they want to look for their own 'life partners' and want to have their own children. In short, they want to create their own families. The relationships of the three daughters with their respective husbands, that develop through the play, are all quite different from each other. Maggie and Will are completely supportive of each other; Albert begins to seem an irrelevance to Alice, as what is more important to her is her social position; Vickey, who is expecting a baby in the later part of the play, is perhaps closer to the 'Hobson' model in that she seems totally reliant on Fred.

The interesting question is raised as to whether or not a child has a lifelong obligation to a parent. In some cultures the answer to this question is certainly 'yes'; Hobson would wish for the same answer, although the daughters may feel differently.

Chauvinism

Chauvinism

One dictionary definition of chauvinism is 'a prejudiced belief in the superiority of one's own group'. The word is frequently linked with the word 'male' to produce the phrase 'male chauvinist', which clearly means when a man believes himself to be superior to women. It is obviously possible to apply this word, and possibly phrase, to Henry Hobson, but it is also possible to apply it to Jim Heeler. It would never occur to either of them that they should take into consideration the women in their families; it is assumed that the women will do as they are told. In fairness to them, this was the prevailing view of the time and the majority of women also accepted it as the norm. During the play, however, this natural order of things is upset and we see male chauvinism overturned, both in the case of Hobson, who has to agree to becoming subservient to the women in his life (most notably Maggie), and in the cases of the younger men who find that equality is expected in their marriages.

Love and marriage

Love and marriage

Three marriages take place in the play, and you must decide whether they will prove to be successful marriages and whether they are based on love. Initially, perhaps, the marriage between Maggie and Willie seems the most unlikely to succeed. It seems to be a marriage of convenience based not on love but on complementary skills: Willie is the bootmaker and Maggie is the bootseller. It becomes evident, though, that a mutual affection is quickly developing and, even though Willie is very uncertain of himself on their marriage night, this affection clearly develops into love. Towards the end of the play we can have no doubt that the marriage will succeed.

The marriage of Vickey and Fred is the most uncomplicated of the three. Vickey clearly accepts the 'normal' type of relationship and slots into a fairly subordinate role in the marriage. She and Fred are almost shy about the relationship at the beginning, and there is clearly a very real and mutual affection. This love blossoms after the marriage, and the family will be complete with the arrival of the baby which will be doted on by two loving parents.

Perhaps the marriage of Alice and Albert is a little more complicated if we try to analyse the feelings of Alice. At the beginning of the play they are the ones who insist that they are in love, and Albert is always at the shop in the hope of being able to further the courtship. Is it a shallow love? Later in the play we discover a snobbish materialism in Alice. We might wonder if, for her, social standing is more important than love. There is certainly a side to her which suggests that she will always be striving to get and keep the upper hand.

Industry (hard work)

Industry

We see a great deal of evidence of the virtue of industry in the play. The very obvious examples are Maggie and Willie, who work incredibly hard from the beginning. Maggie has quite clearly built up and maintained business in the shop by hard work. Willie is most certainly not afraid of hard work in the workshop under the leadership of Tubby, who is also prepared to turn his hand to anything which is necessary. Luck will not play much of a part in the continuing rise of Maggie and Willie, but hard work will, and this is why they will succeed.

Having said that, perhaps the background against which they have been brought up was one where hard work was the norm. We may see Hobson in decline, but he must have worked hard to build up the business initially. His workforce will always find things to do; if there are no boots to make then they will make clogs to stockpile for future selling. The whole atmosphere of the Lancashire which pervades the play is one of hard work.

Generosity

The greatest example of generosity which we see in the play is the generosity of Mrs Hepworth to Maggie and Willie in lending them the capital to set up their shop. This generosity of spirit shows itself not only in that money, but also in the giving of flowers for Maggie's bouquet. Equally, this generosity is appreciated by Maggie and Willie who do not wish to abuse it but wish to pay the money back as quickly as possible, which they do. There are other examples in the play of a complete lack of generosity, exemplified by Alice certainly and Vickey possibly.

Examiner's tips

The **Examiner's tips** found throughout the **Text commentary** and **Exam and coursework practice** sections highlight key points in the text, provide advice on avoiding common errors and offer useful hints on thoroughly preparing yourself for coursework and examination essays on this novel.

■ Text commentary

Act One

At the beginning of the play Maggie, Alice and Vickey, the three daughters of Harold Hobson, are in his shoe shop. Hobson has not appeared, having been at a meeting of the Masons the night before, where he probably had too much to drink. Alice is rather nervous because Albert Prosser is coming to see her as he does every day. Albert arrives but, when he knows that Hobson may appear, he decides not to stay. As he has come into the shop, Maggie insistently sells him a pair of boots even though he doesn't want them. After Albert has left, Hobson appears and says he is popping out for a quarter of an hour, but the girls know that he will probably be a lot longer than that and tell him not to be late for dinner in an hour's time. Hobson objects to their attitude towards him and starts talking of their 'bumptiousness'. Alice and Vickey regard themselves as extremely fashionable, to which Hobson objects as their appearance has been commented on by the pub landlord. He decides that the way to deal with them is to get them married off. Maggie asks about herself getting married, but she is laughed at and told that she is too old.

Mrs Hepworth comes into the shop and wants to know who made her latest pair of shoes; everyone assumes that she is going to complain. It is established that Willie Mossop made them, and Mrs Hepworth gives him her card, as she is in fact very pleased with her shoes and wants Willie to make them for her family, and to let her know if he moves on.

As Mrs Hepworth leaves, Jim Heeler, a friend of Hobson's, comes in and the girls are sent out. Hobson explains that he is concerned about his daughters, and Jim advises marriage, but when he starts talking about 'settlements', Hobson loses interest and they go off to the 'Moonraker's' Inn, Hobson saying he'll be back for dinner.

Maggie calls Willie Mossop up from the workshop. She has decided that she is going to marry Willie, and that they have skills which complement each other. Willie insists that he doesn't love her and that he is 'tokened' to Ada Figgins, his landlady's daughter, but these things are irrelevant to Maggie and are swept aside. When Ada appears with Willie's lunch Maggie shows that Ada is not only very weak, but has no ambition for Willie. Ada is routed but says that her mother will deal with Willie. Willie is clearly afraid of Ada's mother and tries to say that he would prefer to marry Ada. Maggie deals with this by saying that Willie will no longer lodge there, but will lodge at Tubby Wadlow's (the senior shoemaker) and, to make things easier, Tubby will collect Willie's things. Willie is actually quite happy to move away from Ada and her mother. Maggie says that they will be married in three weeks.

When Alice and Vickey come back to be told what is happening, Alice is annoyed as she sees things being spoilt for herself and Albert. When Hobson arrives back and is told about Willie he makes it clear that none of the girls are to be married and packs them off to dinner, but Maggie bars the way and makes it clear that she will want wages of 15s a week to add to Willie's wages or they will go elsewhere. Hobson calls Willie in and threatens to beat the love out of him with his belt. Hobson only hits Willie once and Willie's reaction is to kiss Maggie. Somewhere he has found the strength to make it clear to Hobson that, if he is hit again, he will walk out of the shop with Maggie and they will set up for themselves.

'The shop windows and entrance from street occupy the left side. Facing the audience is the counter ...'

The stage direction at the beginning of Act One is not only long, it goes beyond what is strictly necessary in terms of describing the setting and characters to give us some background to the play. We can divide it into three parts. The first part describes, in detail, the interior of Hobson's shop:

'... Cane chairs in front of counter. There is a desk down left with a chair. A door right leads up to the house. In the centre of the stage is a trap leading to the cellar ...'

This type of stage direction tells a director, and us as readers, exactly what the play should look like on stage. The intention is that the play should be in an absolutely realistic setting. We have already looked at how the play belongs to its period and the set is intended to enhance this.

The second section provides us with additional information which is designed to help us understand the situation in which the characters live and how the general atmosphere of the shop is created:

'The business is prosperous, but to prosper in Salford in 1880 you did not require the accessories of a later day ... The rank and file use the cane chairs in the shop, which is dingy but business-like.'

'Sitting behind the counter are ... Alice, who is twenty-three, and Victoria, who is twenty-one, and very pretty ... The door opens and Maggie enters. She is Hobson's eldest daughter, thirty.'

Family relationships

The third section of the direction introduces us to Henry Horatio Hobson's family:

The discussion which the three daughters have consists of one-line contributions, and they do not seem interested in each other. Maggie is carrying on with her normal work, dealing with the account book. Vickey doesn't stop her reading. The conversation is all about their father who they know will go out as soon as he is up, but until then he makes it impossible for them to do anything other than remain in the positions in which he has placed them.

Industry

Maggie is a very good worker – a successful saleswoman. We feel that there is also a mischievousness at the back of the situation when she sets about selling Albert a pair of boots. She knows exactly why he is there, which is to pursue his relationship with Alice.

Albert's exit allows the girls to talk again, and there is obviously no love lost between them. Alice says to Maggie, who is obviously set apart from the others, 'It's all very well for an old maid like you to talk …', but Maggie responds, 'See that slipper with the fancy buckle on to make it pretty? Courting's like that, my lass. All glitter and no use to nobody.' It is clear that, with no mother and with the age difference between Maggie and the other daughters, Maggie has been performing the maternal role.

As you are reading the play, make sure that you form a first impression of the relationships between the characters and how they interact with each other.

'Hobson … is fifty-five, successful, coarse, florid …'

With Henry Hobson's entrance, we have the whole of the Hobson family together. It is clear that Hobson believes that he is in control of the family situation, but it is equally clear that he really does nothing more than periodically throw his weight around. He is never there. He initially intends to go to the Moonraker's, the public house which is referred to repeatedly in the play and which seems to be more central to his life than either his home or his business. However, he doesn't go to the Moonraker's because he is concerned about his daughters' 'uppishness' and 'bumptiousness'. He is concerned about the name of the family:

Henry Hobson

'I'm warning you your conduct towards your parent's got to change. But that's not all … I speak of public conduct … The fair name and fame of Hobson have been outraged by members of Hobson's family, and uppishness has done it.'

In view of what he is to do himself later in the play, this is almost prophetic, as is his, 'you'll none rule me.'

In the course of the family 'discussion' Maggie points out that they are not paid anything by Hobson for all the work they do in the shop, and it is clear that Hobson believes that he makes the decisions and is in control. The only

Chauvinism

reason that the girls have new clothes is because it is good for trade if they look nice when they're in the shop. If we take their clothes as an example of Hobson's real interest in them though, we find that he relies on Mr Tudsbury the draper to determine what his daughters will wear, and will only complain if he becomes aware of things of which he doesn't approve, as with the bustle which was fashionable at the time. Hobson's solution to any further lack of obedience from his younger daughters is to say that he will marry them off to men of his choosing. It is treated as a joke when Maggie suggests that she may be married as well. When Hobson talks of her being shelved, it is probable that she has been so busy looking after him and her sisters that she has never had the chance before to get married.

'Enter Mrs H, an old lady with a curt manner and good clothes.'

Mrs Hepworth is clearly socially rather above the Hobsons and a very valued

customer, so when she arrives even Hobson himself immediately changes his plans in order to welcome her. He gets down on his knees and grovels around her feet when she refers to the boots she is wearing. Initially Hobson wants to take all possible credit for himself, until he thinks that there might be something wrong when he changes tack: 'But if there is anything wrong I assure you I'm capable of making the man suffer for it.'

It is very noticeable that, during the dialogue, Mrs Hepworth largely ignores Hobson; she believes that she can get more sense out of Maggie, who at last gets the answer from Tubby. Even while she is talking to Willie, Hobson tries to interrupt, only making a further fool of himself in the process. Mrs Hepworth states that she wants only Willie to make her boots and her daughters' boots in future and, and she further insists: '… you won't dare leave here to go to another shop without letting me know where you are.' The seeds have been sown for Willie's future.

> When you are getting the storyline of the play clearly into your mind, make sure that you distinguish the most important key moments in the story and make a special point of learning them and their significance.

'Last time she puts her foot in my shop …'

With every incident it is clear that Hobson is most certainly not in control of anything at all and perhaps, for all his bluster, he is insecure. He threatens to

Henry Hobson

bar Mrs Hepworth from his shop because she has praised Willie to his face, which may make Willie 'uppish'.

Jim Heeler, one of Hobson's friends who now comes in to see him, has far more common sense and tries to tell Hobson that he is going about it all the wrong way if he thinks he is going to solve matters simply by shouting at his daughters. Again the talk returns to marriage but Hobson, in his ignorance, has not considered the potential cost which will have to include settlements for the daughters. At the mention of money Hobson declares that marriages are now off the agenda. Even as he goes out he repeats his futile assertion: 'Dinner will be when I come in for it. I'm master here.'

Make sure that you don't ignore the minor characters in a play; they nearly always have a very important part to play, even if it is only for a few moments, in the action.

'I think you'll do for me.'

It is a spur of the moment decision on the part of Maggie to decide that she

Maggie Hobson

will take the initiative and propose to marry Willie, but when she says: 'I've watched you for a long time and everything I've seen, I've liked … Six months I've counted on you …' we see that she has been considering the idea for some time. It is Mrs Hepworth who has suddenly allowed her to see the future. Maggie and Willie are the same age; they have skills which complement each other. Maggie sees that they could both do better.

Mrs Hepworth

Inevitably Willie is unsure because he does not consider himself to be in love with Maggie, and there is something of the romantic in him which makes him believe that love is essential for a relationship which goes beyond a business partnership. The contrast between the two of them is amusing, with Willie trying to find excuses, and Maggie instantly shooting them down. Ada is just such an excuse, but there are only two reasons why Willie argues for Ada: firstly, she is so inadequate that even in his present situation he feels that he is superior and is needed to protect her; secondly he is afraid of

William Mossop

her mother. If it wasn't such a one-sided affair, Maggie's exchange with Ada Figgins might be quite exciting and passionate, but passion does not come into it; the exchange therefore ends up as being comical with Willie's rather pathetic: 'Seems like there's no escape.'

The fact is though, that Willie does not want to escape and it is with terrific relief that he embraces the news that he will not have to go back to the Figgins' at all. He is delighted that Maggie is sorting everything out for him, it is just that he has problems coping with the speed of change. He needs at this point to escape back down into the cellar.

'Marry – you – Mossop!'

Family relationships

The reaction of the family to the engagement has nothing at all to do with Maggie's happiness or with Willie; it has to do with their perception of what effect such a relationship will have on their own lives. Alice is concerned that it will spoil her chances with Albert. Hobson shows himself to be a snob when he comments on Willie's father having been a 'workhouse brat', but it is really that he is afraid others will laugh at him. He shows once again an inability to cope with anything in a rational way, his reaction being to call Willie up from the cellar and to start beating him with the leather belt which he has taken from around his waist. Whatever the conventions may have been of the Victorian father or the Victorian employer, we must remember that both Maggie and Willie are thirty years old. Willie shows that underneath he has considerable strength of character, and ironically the leather belt is the spur which is needed to make him take the lead in his relationship with Maggie. '... if Mr Hobson raises up that strap again, I'll do more. I'll walk straight out of shop with thee and us two 'ull set up for ourselves.'

This response may surprise us; it may surprise Hobson; it probably surprises Willie himself, but it doesn't surprise Maggie: 'Willie! I knew you had it in you, lad.'

■ Self-test questions Act One

Uncover the plot
1 Why is Hobson getting up late?
2 Why does Albert want to leave almost as soon as he arrives?
3 Why is it significant that Hobson says he hates lawyers?
4 What is Hobson's 'business appointment'?
5 How does Hobson describe a bustle?
6 Why does Maggie call Tubby up to speak to Mrs Hepworth?
7 Who made Mrs Hepworth's boots?
8 Why does Mrs Hepworth give Willie her card?
9 What does Mrs Hepworth compare Willie to?
10 Why does she make this comparison?
11 Why doesn't Hobson like Mrs Hepworth praising Willie to his face?
12 What is the evidence that Hobson is a good orator?

33

13 When Hobson says he wants his daughters to wed 'temperance young men', what does temperance mean?

14 What does Hobson mean when he says, 'I'll get me hand down for the wedding all right'?

15 Willie is 'tokened' – what does this mean?

16 How does Maggie know who Ada is?

17 What does Willie think of Mrs Figgins?

18 If Willie is not going to live at the Figgins', where will he live?

19 How will Maggie protect Will from Mrs Figgins?

20 How would you describe Maggie and Willie's first kiss?

Who said that, and to whom?

1 'This is a shop, you know. We're not here to let people go out without buying.'

2 'Interfering with my goings out and comings in. The idea! I've a mind to take measures with the lot of you.'

3 'I'm British middle class and proud of it.'

4 'But if you want the brutal truth, you're past the marrying age.'

5 'I wish some people would mind their own business.'

6 'You're a natural born genius at making boots. It's a pity you're a natural fool at all else.'

7 'It's a puzzle to me all ways.'

8 'I'd be the laughing-stock of the place if I allowed it.'

9 'I'll take her quick, aye, and stick to her like glue.'

10 'I knew you had it in you, lad.'

Take your time questions

These three questions on Act One begin to explore the types of question that you might be asked in your GCSE examinations. They are of different types: the first asks you to carry out some research. It is also the type of question some of you will explore if you are following a course in GCSE drama. The second question is asking for close textual analysis. The third is asking you to write in a way that recreates an idea from the play, but you must show an understanding of character and plot as well as using your imagination to answer this question.

1 Examine the stage directions in Act One and:
   i)   draw the set (or, if art is not your strong point, draw a simple plan and describe it in your own words);
   ii) research clothes of the 1880s and either draw several costume designs or describe your costume ideas in detail;
   iii) write a paragraph explaining in your own words why *Hobson's Choice* belongs in its period.

2 Reread the section in Act One beginning with Vickey saying, 'We shall dress as we like ...' and ending with Alice saying, 'We shall continue to dress fashionably, father.' Explain in your own words what Hobson is trying to say about their clothes.

3 Use what we know from reading the play and your imagination to describe a typical day in Maggie's life.

Act Two

The story moves on to a month later when we find that Tubby is in the shop with Alice and Vickey. He is asking what should be done in the workshop as there are no orders

for shoes, the high-class trade having dropped off. He asks if he should make clogs, although he is aware that there is very little profit in clogs. Alice has no idea what to do and wonders what Maggie would have done in these circumstances. At this point Maggie and Willie come in on their way to their wedding. They have with them Freddie Beenstock, who is interested in courting Vickey. Maggie sends Freddie to fetch Albert. Apparently Hobson is sleeping in the cellar at Beenstock's grain warehouse, having fallen down an open trap in the pavement onto a pile of grain sacks; he isn't hurt.

In the course of the conversation it becomes clear that Maggie and Willie have their own shop which is proving to be a success. Alice and Vickey are, of course, very interested in where the money came from to start the business, but this is not clarified. Maggie and Willie are working in two cellars, and will be living there as well once they are married. They have called by to collect some broken furniture from the lumber room which Willie will mend. Alice and Vickey begin to realise that, although they may not approve of her choice of husband, Maggie will at least be married with a home of her own. Maggie makes it clear that she will help Alice and Vickey marry the men they would like, but first they must come to her wedding. Maggie's plan is that Hobson will be served with a writ for trespass which Albert has drawn up. Freddie is sent to place the writ on the sleeping Hobson. Albert, to his surprise, is sent with the handcart to deliver the furniture to the cellars. Then they all go off to the wedding, leaving Tubby in charge of the shop.

'Alice is in Maggie's chair at the desk ... Vickey is reading behind the counter ... Tubby stands near the desk by Alice.'

The stage direction at the beginning of Act Two is short. We are told that there has been a passage of time, but the setting has not changed and we already know the characters. The only difference is their positions. It is established immediately that in the month which has passed the business has gone downhill very fast. Clogs can be made to increase the stock, but there are no orders at all for high-class boots. Tubby makes it clear that without the high-class trade Hobson won't even be able to pay the rent on the shop, let alone any profit. Tubby does not want to make any decision about what is to be done, and wants Alice to make the decision. She doesn't know what to do: 'Oh dear! What would Miss Maggie have told you to do?' In the end it is quite a petulant decision on her part: 'Then go and make clogs.'

As soon as Tubby has gone, Alice begins to doubt whether she has made

the right decision and Vickey is no help at all. Alice's basic problem is that she is simply not up to the job, which becomes very clear when she admits that she cannot add up. They both try to insist that it is not their job to run the shop, but Hobson's. This discussion allows Vickey to give us the very important piece of information that, since Maggie's departure, Hobson has spent more time than ever at the Moonraker's: 'He ought to look after his business himself instead of wasting more time than ever in the "Moonraker's".'

The other piece of information we are given early in this act is that Vickey has a young man, Freddie Beenstock. Immediately after this revelation we meet the young man in question as he comes in with Maggie and Willie. The stage direction tells us that Maggie and Willie are about to be married and that it is going to be a simple affair, with no dressing up. Why Freddie is with them we are not immediately told, but we are told that he is a smart-looking, respectable tradesman.

Alice: 'I don't know what you're aiming at, Maggie, but –'
Maggie: 'The difference between us is that I do. I always did.'

The minute she arrives Maggie takes complete command of the situation and everyone else seems inadequate. She knows that Freddie is interested in Vickey; she knows her father has got worse since she and Willie left; she knows where her father is and exactly how to deal with the situation. What Maggie has come to deal with are the marriages of her two sisters. In Act One Hobson had said they were to be married; the fact that he changed his mind is irrelevant: 'I don't allow for folks to change their minds.'

As you work through the play, select a few quotations which, for you, best illustrate each of the characters. Don't make them too long. Don't choose too many. Mark them in the text and either learn them or make sure that you know where to find them quickly.

Alice and Vickey are convinced still that Maggie's marriage to Willie Mossop has spoilt their chances of marrying as he is beneath them, but Maggie insists that he is welcomed into the family, and that he kisses her sisters. This turns into a rather amusing moment. With Vickey, Maggie says, 'Protest but kiss.' With Alice there is rather more prevarication, and she says that she will do it if Maggie helps her with the books. She gets no help, but kisses Willie, who decides he rather likes kissing young women.

After the kissing there is just a moment when Alice tries to behave with Maggie as Maggie had behaved towards Albert – Maggie is in the shop so Alice tries to sell her something. When Maggie responds slightly incredulously, Alice immediately re-phrases what she is saying into a simple question asking Maggie what she is doing there. Maggie tells her sisters that it is her wedding day and she expects her sisters to be both at the church and at the 'wedding-spread' in the evening.

Vickey clearly wants to say that she won't come, as coming will mean that she has given her approval but, as Maggie says, kissing the bridegroom has signified approval anyway. The sisters then try to use the shop as an excuse but Maggie knows the situation in the shop and, since business is very slow, Tubby can look after the shop.

Vickey and Fred

'Willie and me aren't throwing our money around, but we can pay our way.'

One thing Maggie does want to buy from the shop, which appals her sisters,

is a brass ring out of stock, to use as a wedding ring. It costs fourpence and she reminds Alice to enter the price in the ledger. At this point Maggie and Willie have no money. They have started to furnish their rooms with second-hand furniture which they have bought from the market. In a sense Maggie wants the disapproval of her sisters so that there is no argument about taking some bits of old furniture out of the lumber

Love and marriage

room. Maggie and Willie have brought a handcart with them, and Willie immediately takes his coat off and his cuffs, ready to go upstairs and bring the things down. Alice is worried that they are going to take things out of her room (that used to be Maggie's), but they only take a couple of broken chairs and a sofa with the springs all gone. The disapproval of her sisters doesn't worry Maggie at all, and her confidence in the future is clear: 'And when me and Will are richer than the lot of you together, it'll be grand satisfaction to look back and think about how we were when we began.'

'… all I'm taking off you is some crippled stuff that isn't yours and what I'm getting for you is marriage portions.'

It is almost inevitable that, when the chairs appear, the sisters see possible uses

for them, but Maggie insists on taking them as her due, pointing out that, although the sisters don't understand, she is in the process of arranging marriage portions for them. As ever Maggie is in complete control of the situation: Alice and Vickey are sent to put their hats on. Albert and Freddie arrive. Freddie is immediately despatched, minus his coat, to help

Maggie Hobson

Willie with the sofa. Albert produces a legal paper. Maggie is quite contemptuous of all the legal jargon, but Albert explains that it is exactly what she has asked for, an action against Hobson for trespass and for 'spying on the trade secrets of the aforesaid J.B. and Co'. Initially the accusation seems ridiculous, and we would agree with Albert who would not want to go into court with the paper, but that is not the purpose of the paper.

It is essential when you are studying a play to make sure that you get the storyline very clearly in your mind, as you will need to know it to be able to answer examination questions properly. However, weak answers tell too much of the story.

Willie and Freddie appear with the sofa. Albert opens the door and they take it out to put it on the cart. Time has passed and Maggie now gives out a flurry of orders as they are in danger of being late at the church. Her sisters are to come down now. Willie and Freddie are to put their coats back on. Freddie is to go and put the legal paper on the sleeping Hobson. He is then to go on to the church. Albert has to take the handcart to Oldfield Road. He protests about this, but in the end he goes. Tubby is called up to take charge of the shop. They are ready to go to the church.

Just before they go we see an important sincerity in Maggie. She needs to

Love and marriage

know that Willie wants to marry her: 'Yon's not the place for lies. The parson's going to ask you will you have me and you'll either answer truthfully or not at all. If you're not willing, just say so now, and —', but Willie reassures her: 'You're growing on me, lass. I'll toe the line with you.' And so they go off to their wedding with Tubby throwing old shoes after them for luck.

■ Self-test questions Act Two

Uncover the plot

1   What do we gather has happened to business at Hobson's?
2   Why does Tubby say they can always make clogs?
3   Which of the daughters finally makes the decision about what Tubby should do?
4   What is the basic problem Alice has with the books?
5   What does Vickey reveal to Alice?
6   When Maggie arrives why is she so sure that Hobson won't arrive?
7   Where is Willie's shop?
8   When Alice knows about the shop, what is her first question?
9   What does Maggie make Alice and Vickey do?
10   When and where do Maggie and Willie get married?
11   What does Vickey sell Maggie?
12   What does Willie take off before he goes to the lumber room?
13   What do Willie and Maggie take from the lumber room?
14   Why do Maggie and Willie need furniture quickly?
15   What has Albert brought with him when he arrives at the shop?
16   What is Fred sent to do before going to the church?

17 What is Albert sent to do?
18 While they all go to the wedding, who is in charge of the shop?
19 Willie talks about going to the church in such a way that it sounds as if he is going somewhere else. Where?
20 What does Tubby throw after Willie and Maggie?

Who said that, and to whom?
1 'I'm not snappy in myself … It's these figures. I can't get them right.'
2 'I'm here to help you if you'll have my help.'
3 'the difference between us is that I do. I always did.'
4 'I don't allow for folks to change their minds.'
5 'It's under protest.'
6 'Where's your pride gone to …'
7 '… I'll leave the lot of you to tackle this yourselves and a nice hash you'll make of it.'
8 'Suppose some of my friends see me?'
9 'It's church we're going to, not the dentists.'
10 'Do you think I'd trust him to remember?'

Take your time questions
1 Imagine you are Hobson, and describe your walk home from the Moonraker's on that fateful night.
2 Now that you are at the end of Act Two you should be able to put a substantial part of a character study of Maggie together. Write this preliminary character study.
3 One of the themes we are studying is 'family relationships'. Write about how snobbery affects, or threatens to affect relationships in the Hobson family.

Act Three

The wedding is over and everyone is back at the cellars in Oldfield Road for the wedding breakfast, sitting on the repaired furniture, with a large pork pie and a small cake to eat. Willie makes a well-made and generous speech. Everyone still wants to know how Maggie and Willie raised the money for their shop but, although they admit that they had help, they go no further, except to say that Maggie's bouquet of hot-house flowers came from the same place. The girls need to go back to Hobson's shop, and Willie is told to wash up. When Freddie and Albert laugh at him they find that they have to help as well. The girls go to put on their hats and Albert and Freddie attempt to help Willie, but they are not much use. Willie would like the guests to stay as he is a little nervous of his wedding night. When the girls come back Maggie takes over the clearing up. At this point Hobson arrives knocking on the door. Alice, Vickey, Albert and Freddie are sent into the bedroom while Maggie and Willie speak to Hobson.

Hobson is greeted as a wedding guest, but of course he has not come for the wedding; he has come because he is in trouble and wants to talk something over with Maggie. Hobson produces the action for damages for trespass, and tries to blame Maggie and Willie for the fact that he stayed at the Moonraker's too long. Maggie persistently asks if it was an accident or trespass, and Hobson insists that it was an accident. All he sees is that it is going to cost him money, and that the incident will get into the paper, thus bringing more shame on him, and if he has to resign as church warden, he won't get the trade from the church members. He cannot bring himself to accept advice from Willie, but Maggie says that as the thing he is most afraid of is appearing in court, he must attempt to settle things out of court, in private. Maggie then calls Albert from the bedroom and introduces him as Prosser the lawyer, and also calls Fred Beenstock out. Albert and Fred ask Hobson for a thousand pounds, but Maggie is still very firmly in control and makes it clear that Hobson can only afford five hundred pounds. When Hobson has agreed to this it is revealed that Alice and Vickey are going to marry Albert and Freddie, at which point Hobson loses his temper and leaves. The others also leave, promising that they will let Maggie and Willie know when the weddings will take place. Maggie is sure that in twenty years' time Willie will be more highly thought of than his brothers-in-law. Willie gets on with his writing. Maggie finishes clearing away and, in doing so, refers to the flowers as 'Mrs Hepworth's', sentimentally keeping one flower to be pressed in her bible.

Maggie then goes to bed while Willie continues with his writing. When he has finished he shows his continuing nervousness, takes off his boots and collar and lies down on the settee. Maggie appears and drags him by the ear into the bedroom.

'The cellar at Oldfield Road is at once workroom, shop, and living-room …'

For Act Three the scene has changed and consequently there is a fairly lengthy stage direction which describes the new setting. As at the beginning of Act One, the description is quite precise. For instance there are three windows high up at the back, each one identical to the others. There are seven stairs down into the cellar. There is a small screen hiding the sink, and there is a door to the second cellar which is used as a bedroom. It is made clear that the cellar is workroom, shop and sitting room all at the same time. Willie's bench and tools are up against one wall; the chairs and sofa, now mended, are in another part of the room.

'It's a very great pleasure to us to see you here tonight.'

The occasion is the wedding breakfast, which has consisted of pork pie,

Family relationships

wedding cake and a pot of tea. The health of the bride and bridegroom is drunk in tea. It is a happy occasion, even if rather cramped with all four guests sitting on the sofa. Maggie and Willie have the chairs and, at the beginning of the scene, Willie rises to make his speech. He is predictably nervous but, after one pause, he makes the speech without any problems.

The toast that he proposed is kind and generous: 'Our guests, and may they all be married soon themselves.' Albert is not allowed by Alice to reply to the toast for several reasons: in the first place he has already made a speech; we know from what Willie has said that he proposed the toast to the bride and groom. Alice also makes the point that there has been too much speech making, but when Albert prevaricates the real reason comes out: 'But you'll not speak as well as he did, so we can leave it with a good wind-up.'

'I'm free to own you took me by surprise, Will.'

Love and marriage

All the guests make it clear that they are impressed with the progress Willie has made. His education is progressing, and Maggie again says that she believes Willie will be a considerable success. Like Alice, Albert tries to find out where the capital came from to set them up in 'Snug little rooms. Shop of your own. And so on.' Maggie makes the point that it is Willie's shop, but her explanation, 'He's the saving sort', is clearly inadequate.

We are beginning to see Willie's character develop. For further discussion on the development of his character see the example question on page 52 and the outline answer on page 54.

Alice is concerned to get back home because she is nervous that Hobson may have returned. The girls go to put their hats on, and on her way out Maggie asks Willie to clear the table. Freddie and Albert laugh at this, but Maggie does not like people laughing at Willie, so she tells them that they have to help with the clearing up too. They agree to help because they must keep on the right side of Maggie, at least until after they are married. Willie is keen for Albert and Freddie to stay because this will be the first time that he has been alone with Maggie outside working hours and he is rather nervous at the prospect: 'I'd be deeply obliged if you would stay on for a bit to help to – to thaw the ice for me … Maggie's not the sort you get familiar with.' Albert and Freddie find this extremely amusing and are not willing to help him out: 'It's not our job to do your melting for you.'

Maggie and her sisters come back in, and then there is a knock at the door

Family relationships

– it becomes clear that it is Hobson who is knocking. Maggie's sisters, and their young men are frightened of what Hobson will say when he finds them there. Maggie sends them into the bedroom to await the time when they will be needed. Her sisters would rather not be needed at all, but Maggie makes the decisions, although she says to Willie: 'You sit you still, and don't forget you're the gaffer here', and when Hobson says he'll come in Maggie says, 'Well, I don't know. I'll have to ask the master about that.'

'It wasn't sociability that brought me, Maggie.'

Maggie and Willie pretend that they don't know why Hobson has arrived and

Henry Hobson

offer him stewed tea, pork pie and wedding cake, none of which he wants – he has a dreadful hangover and he is only concerned for himself, but Maggie will not listen to him until he has eaten the wedding cake because, as she says: 'I'm quite aware it's foolishness, but I've a wish to see my father sitting at my table eating my wedding cake on my wedding-day.'

Hobson eats the cake and drinks the tea and then thinks that he will be able to discuss things with Maggie.

To his surprise, however, Maggie makes to go and leave him with Willie,

Chauvinism

her argument being that business needs to be discussed between men: ' … you can discuss it man to man with no fools of women about.' Hobson accepts that Willie will stay and after passing the paper to him via Maggie, Hobson adopts what is probably his normal public speaking haranguing of his audience. However, Maggie interrupts him and asks the

straightforward question, 'Did you trespass?' Hobson gives her a straight answer but tells her that it is all her fault. The reason Hobson stayed too long in the Moonraker's and got drunk is because he was trying to forget his thankless child. He admits he fell into the cellar and fell asleep. Hobson insists it was an accident, but reveals his terror of lawyers: 'I've kept away from lawyers all my life, I've hated lawyers … They'll squeeze me dry for it.'

'I'm getting a lot of comfort from your husband Maggie.'

Hobson continues to blame Maggie and Willie, who doesn't help matters with

William Mossop

his naive question: 'Do you think it will get into the paper, Maggie?' Hobson then sees the potential disaster of appearing in the newspapers, and again Willie's comment doesn't help matters: 'Other people's troubles is mostly what folks read the paper for, and I reckon it's twice the pleasure to them when it's trouble of a man they know themselves.' The stage

direction is important here as it indicates both how the lines should be said and the simplicity of Willie's character: 'He is perfectly simple and has no malicious intention.'

'Now about this accident of yours.'

Maggie Hobson

Maggie now takes control again and suggests that matters could be settled out of court, without publicity. It will cost Hobson something to settle, but she points out that is inevitable. She can now produce all the occupants of the bedroom who are relevant to the case. Hobson has problems coping with the situation and feels that his brain is giving way.

The only thing he can grasp at is that the shop has been left attended only by Tubby and he starts blustering at Alice and Vickey. He is stopped in his tracks by Maggie, who reminds him that her sisters have been at her wedding.

It is now time for Albert to play his role as lawyer, which he begins to do

very effectively with Hobson digging a deeper and deeper hole for himself with his attitude. Hobson does, however, cut short the legal jargon with the simple question, 'How much?' Albert tries for a thousand pounds, but we again see that he is not actually in control of the situation when Maggie interrupts. The figure that she has decided on is five hundred pounds, which she knows her father can afford.

'I'll run that shop with men ...'

Hobson realises that he has been duped, but there is nothing that he can do

Chauvinism

about it; his two other daughters will marry, with marriage portions of two hundred and fifty pounds each. Hobson's reaction is, in the first place, interestingly chauvinistic in that he decides the shop will now be run by men. He then makes a comment to Willie: 'Will Mossop ... you're the best of the bunch. You're a backward lad, but you know your trade and it's an honest one.' He then declares himself free and leaves for the Moonraker's. Alice and Albert, Vickey and Freddie can now go and arrange their weddings.

As Alice goes she acknowledges what Maggie has done for them when she

Industry

thanks her. Once again there is reference to the progress which Maggie intends she and Willie to make: '...only don't come round here too much, because Will and me's going to be busy.' When the others have gone and it is time for Willie's lesson we learn that the sentence he was practising the previous night was, 'There is always room at the top' and the sentence for this, his wedding night is, 'Great things grow from small'.

While Willie continues his writing practice, Maggie finishes clearing up.

Maggie Hobson

Her bouquet of flowers has to go, but there is a moment of sentiment which shows us another side of Maggie when she takes a single flower to press it in her bible as a keepsake of the day which has been very important to her. She then decides, possibly for the only time in her life, that she will leave the pots until morning as she is tired.

Willie finishes his writing and the scene ends with a moment of humour. Willie takes off his boots but looks nervously at the bedroom door before he lies down on the sofa. Maggie emerges in a night-dress, with a candle and takes him by the ear, leading him into the bedroom.

Don't just accept other people's opinions of the characters. Your teacher will interpret the characters during the course of lessons. Books such as this one will interpret the characters in a particular way. Always look at the characters and decide for yourself what you actually think of them – your view may differ in some respects from what you have read or have been told. As long as you can justify your opinion then it is not wrong.

■ Self-test questions Act Three

Uncover the plot
1 There are two reasons why Alice doesn't want Albert to speak after Willie. What are they?
2 What does Alice still want to know about the shop?
3 What clue are they given about Alice's enquiry?
4 What is Willie told to do while Maggie is out?
5 Why do Albert and Freddie decide to help with the washing up?
6 Why does Willie want Albert and Freddie to stay?
7 Who knocks at the door?
8 Before the door is opened where does Maggie send Alice, Vickey, Albert and Freddie?
9 What is Hobson offered to drink?
10 Why does Maggie make Hobson eat the cake?
11 Why does Maggie offer to leave?
12 Why has Hobson come to the cellars?
13 Who does Hobson try to blame for his dilemma?
14 Which two newspapers does Hobson think might print the story?
15 Hobson is frightened he will lose what position?
16 Why is Albert called out first?
17 How much does Albert try to claim from Hobson as an out-of-court settlement?
18 How much does Maggie say will be paid?
19 What is the money for?
20 What are the two sentences which Willie is learning to write?

Who said that, and to whom?
1 '… you've had one turn and you needn't start again.'
2 'If we start giving in to her now she'll be a nuisance to us all our lives.'
3 'You sit still, and don't forget you're the gaffer here.'
4 'A sore and sad misfortune's fallen on me.'
5 'Other people's troubles is mostly what folks read the paper for …'
6 'Honest men live by business and lawyers live by law.'
7 'It's not going out of the family, father.'
8 'I've suffered thirty years and more and I'm a free man from today.'
9 'We're only starting here.'
10 'There is always room at the top.'

Take your time questions
1 At the end of Act Two you wrote a preliminary character study of Maggie. By the end of Act Three Willie's character has developed a lot. Write a preliminary character study of Willie.

2 Although she only appears in Act One, Mrs Hepworth remains very important in the play. Explain in detail, in your own words, the part she plays and why she is important.

3 For Act Three the scene has changed. As for Act One:
   i) draw the set (or draw a simple plan and describe it in your own words);
   ii) research shoes of the period and describe the shoes that Willie might be making;
   iii) write a paragraph describing how you think Willie and Maggie have built up their business.

Act Four

A year later in Hobson's living room Tubby is cooking bacon at the fire for Hobson's breakfast. Jim Heeler comes in (Tubby has sent for him and for a doctor). Clearly, in Hobson's shop, everything is going to rack and ruin as there is no work coming in, the business being reduced to the production of cheap clogs. 'Temper and obstinacy' are ruining everything according to Tubby – the trade has gone to Willie and Maggie. Hobson, hopelessly depressed and hinting at thoughts of suicide, comes in unshaven and without a collar; he knows that his problem is the drink.

Jim is ordered out by the rather blunt doctor, who looks at Hobson and quickly diagnoses chronic alcoholism. The doctor gives Hobson a prescription but, more importantly prescribes no drink. Hobson tries to defy the doctor, pay him and go off to the Moonraker's. The doctor is firm, however, and asks if there is anyone who can keep an eye on Hobson, and when Maggie is mentioned, the doctor decides to go and see her. He doesn't want Maggie to pity Hobson but to discipline him.

At precisely that moment Maggie comes in as Tubby has fetched her (for which Hobson says Tubby is sacked). The doctor explains the situation to Maggie and says that he wants her to return to live at the shop. Maggie says that it is not her decision. She sends Tubby to get the prescription made up and to tell Willie to come round quickly. Hobson wants to know if Maggie is going to come back but she says, to Hobson's astonishment, that she must ask Will, and she will only move back if Willie says that it is her duty; Hobson's bullying will do no good at all.

Alice comes in and, referring to herself as a fashionable solicitor's wife, makes it clear that she has no intention at all of coming back to the shop. Vickey comes in effusively, but she cannot possibly return as she is expecting a child. Vickey and Alice are all for Maggie and Willie coming back to live at the shop, but they then become worried that Hobson may leave all his money to them.

Willie arrives and they find him checking the stock; clearly he is doing well. Alice and Vickey learn that Willie cannot be bossed around and, if he and Maggie are to come back to the shop, he will be doing the arranging and it will be on his terms. Willie greets Hobson rather abruptly, and Alice and Vickey are told to go. Hobson makes a rather desperate attempt to take charge by magnanimously telling Maggie and Willie that they can have the back bedroom, that Maggie can keep house and lend a hand in the shop, and Willie can have his old job back at his old wage. Willie starts to leave, stating that he has a business to run and he's clearly wasting his time with Hobson.

He acknowledges that his business is in a cellar, but says that Mrs Hepworth has been paid back and they have made money. All the high-class trade is with them and all Hobson sells is clogs. Willie will only come back as Hobson's partner, but with Hobson as a sleeping partner with no influence. The shop will be called Mossop and Hobson, and alterations will be made. It becomes very clear that Willie is in control and that things will stay that way.

'The scene represents Hobson's living-room ...'

The stage direction at the beginning of Act Four describes what is the third setting of the play, Hobson's living-room. There has been a shift of time, and certain aspects of the description indicate that things have changed from a year previously. Things aren't quite right – the room is dirty, and Tubby is cooking bacon at the fire. This indicates a change in circumstances, as Tubby should not be doing this at all and is described as 'a puzzled and incompetent amateur'.

'Mr Hobson's not his old self, and the shop's not its own self...'

Jim Heeler's arrival at the very beginning of the scene allows Tubby to fill us

Industry

in with what has been going on in the year that has passed. Hobson has clearly become increasingly difficult, as we see by the contradictory messages he gives: to get the doctor, to get Jim Heeler, that he is getting up, that he wants his breakfast. The fact that Tubby has stuck with Hobson shows a loyalty that is regarded by many as silly. He is clearly a good workman – he trained Willie – but he is no longer able to demonstrate his skills at Hobson's as all he does is make clogs to stockpile. The talk in the town is that Willie has led to Hobson's ruin, but Tubby says that it is 'temper and obstinacy' that have been his downfall. Willie may have taken the trade, but Tubby insists that they could have recovered in time if things had been approached properly. He refers to the male assistants in the shop who are no help at all, and are wrong in every way: they have to be paid higher wages; male customers prefer to be served by female assistants; high-class women prefer to be served by other women.

'Enter Hobson, unshaven, without collar.'

Henry Hobson

With the background now established, Hobson comes in. He is in a hopeless state of depression. Inevitably what Tubby has done is wrong; he doesn't want the bacon and Tubby should be working in the shop. Before he goes Tubby offers to go and fetch Maggie. In his welter of self-pity Hobson agrees in an amusingly melodramatic fashion: 'Oh, go for her. Go for the Devil. What does it matter who you go for? I'm a dying man.' Hobson explains that he is dirty and unwashed because, 'The only use I saw for water was to drown myself ... I've thrown my razor through the window ... or I'd have cut my throat.'

What Hobson does recognise, even before the doctor arrives, is that the cause of his problems is his heavy drinking. Jim Heeler tries to deny this and encourage him. When Dr Macfarlane arrives he is blunt, to the point, and almost a caricature doctor, but he understands from the moment he comes in what Hobson's problem is. The most telling thing which the doctor says to Hobson is: 'Your complaint and your character are the same.' In other words, Hobson has become a chronic alcoholic because of the sort of person he is. Hobson's reaction to the doctor writing a prescription and forbidding him to drink shows the absurdity of his attitude: 'I won't take it. None of your druggist's muck for me …' The doctor threatens to commit him to a lunatic asylum, but Hobson continues to argue: 'I've had my liquor for as long as I remember, and I'll have it to the end.'

However, Hobson has met his match in the doctor, who will not give up on him. He wants to know if Hobson has a wife, and when he is told that she is dead he wants to know if there is a female relative who can 'manage' him.

From what Hobson says, the doctor concludes that Maggie is the one who

Maggie Hobson

is needed to deal with Hobson, and he is prepared to go and fetch Maggie himself: 'If she's the woman I take her for ye'll get no pity. Ye'll get discipline.' Almost immediately Maggie arrives – Tubby has fetched her. Maggie is told very clearly by the doctor what the situation is and what the three elements of the possible cure are. In the first place Hobson must take the medicine the doctor has prescribed; in the second he must abstain completely from alcohol; in the third Maggie must come and discipline her father. Maggie listens, but insists that the doctor will not make up her mind for her – she will make her own mind up with Willie there to help her.

'I don't want to come father … But if Willie tells me it's my duty I shall come.'

Family relationships

Alice and Albert

Hobson still cannot understand that Maggie will consult Willie before making a decision; he assumes Maggie is in command and is rude about Willie and where they live, which annoys Maggie. Alice, when she arrives, is no help to Maggie, referring to herself as 'a fashionable solicitor's wife'. Alice tells her father how well he is looking; being so wrapped up in herself she doesn't notice anything about anyone else. Her immediate reaction to the news of her father's illness is that she certainly cannot 'come back to this after what I've been used to lately.'

When Vickey arrives Hobson immediately sees her as his saviour, but she claims that she is unable to look after him because she is now pregnant. As Maggie has probably known all along, it is going to be down to her to look after Hobson.

She tells him to get ready for Will's arrival by putting on a collar, which he does, saying, 'But understand me, Maggie, it's not for the sake of Will Mossop. It's because my neck is cold.'

With Hobson out of the way Maggie asks again who is going to come and

look after Hobson. She is met with flat refusals from her sisters, so she says that it is up to Willie. Vickey replies: 'If Alice and I don't need to ask our husbands, I'm sure you never need ask yours. Will Mossop hasn't the spirit of a louse and we know it as well as you do', which is interesting in respect of her attitude to her own husband, but is also preparing us to meet a rather different Willie to the one we are familiar with.

When you are looking at relationships between characters look carefully for the differences which make the characters clearly distinguishable. Those subtle differences, such as those between the attitudes of the three daughters to their husbands, are what make the characters real.

Willie arrives in the shop and Maggie goes to him. This gives Alice and Vickey the chance to discuss what really concerns them: Hobson's money. They are afraid that he will leave what they see as their inheritances to Maggie and Willie. They then discover a very prosperous Willie looking over the stock. He tells them a few home truths, including that Hobson's business is worth almost nothing: 'Stock and goodwill 'ud fetch about two hundred.'

'… if I'm to come into a thing I like to know what I'm coming into.'

Willie clearly knows what he is talking about and Alice and Vickey don't, and

they are not going to get anywhere trying to browbeat Willie. He is in charge. His comment to Vickey in response to one of her attempted snide comments shows this: 'I know Maggie and me gave both of you a big leg up when we arranged your marriage portions, but I dunno that we're grudging you the sudden lift you got.'

In a play of this type it is essential that you are able to believe in the characters, and so you should always ask yourself, 'Is the character real?' If you are able to answer yes, then go on to consider what makes the character real for you. If the answer is no, then go on to consider why you can't believe in the character. You must be able to justify your point of view.

Hobson comes in and Willie takes a 'high hand' with him. Alice and Vickey try to intervene, but they are finally put in their places by Hobson who effectively throws them out, knowing that his only hope lies in Maggie and Willie. Once they have gone Hobson makes his final attempt to take charge. He offers Maggie and Willie the back bedroom, a half share in the rest of the house, Maggie can housekeep and help in the shop and Willie can have his old job back. Willie immediately makes as if to go with Maggie.

Hobson has to be made to see that the business in Oldfield Road may be

Industry

Mrs Hepworth

in two cellars, but it is a huge success. Willie tells him that Mrs Hepworth has been paid back and, although we have had suspicions all along that she lent the capital, this is the first time Hobson will have been told. The high-class trade all comes to Oldfield Road and Hobson sells nothing but clogs. Willie makes Hobson the offer of closing his premises and transferring his business to Hobson's shop; he will allow Hobson a half-share in the business on the condition that Hobson is a sleeping partner. Maggie agrees with this; the only argument is over the name of the shop. 'William Mossop – late Hobson' is rejected by Maggie; 'Hobson and Mossop' is rejected by Willie; 'Mossop and Hobson' is agreed. Willie immediately has plans for improving the shop, including carpet on the floor and comfortable leather chairs for customers to sit on, both concepts which Hobson can't understand. Willie's ambition is clear. Hobson then goes to get his hat so that he can be taken to have the deed of partnership drawn up.

Love and marriage

Willie and Maggie are immensely proud of each other, and have a genuine love for each other which is a love of equals. Willie wants to buy Maggie a gold wedding ring and, although she has no objection to this, she will not take the brass ring off because, as she says, it is important that it will always remind them where they came from.

The play ends with them all leaving for the lawyers with Willie being the last to go. The final stage direction sums the situation up:

'*Will comes down with amazement, triumph and incredulity written on his face and attempts to express the inexpressible by saying –*

Willie: Well, by gum! *(He turns to follow the others.)*'

Remember that Hobson's Choice is a play. If you get the chance to go and see it in the theatre make sure you take the opportunity.

There is a very good old film of the play which stars Sir John Mills as Willie Mossop – try and get hold of a copy on video and watch it.

Visit a museum to get the period feel of the play.

As with all plays do everything you can to make it real for yourself.

Self-test questions Act Four

Uncover the plot

1 There are three pictures on the walls of Hobson's living room. Two of them are of the Queen and Prince Albert. Who's is the third one of? (Find out who he is.)
2 What is Tubby having to do for Hobson?
3 What, according to Tubby, is ruining the shop?
4 What is wrong with the new shop assistants?
5 Who does Tubby want to fetch?
6 Why hasn't Hobson washed and shaved?
7 Why does Dr Macfarlane question that he has been sent for?
8 What has to happen before the doctor will speak properly to Hobson?
9 What is the diagnosis?
10 Why does the doctor refuse his fee?
11 As well as the mixture, what else does the doctor prescribe?
12 Dr Macfarlane doesn't want Maggie to pity Hobson. What does he want her to do?
13 Why doesn't Alice want to come back to look after her father?
14 Why does Vickey claim she can't come and look after Hobson?
15 What worries Alice and Vickey most about the possibility of Maggie and Willie living back at Hobson's?
16 Why does Willie speak in the way he does?
17 What does Willie finally reveal when he is telling Hobson what he and Maggie have achieved?
18 What does Willie insist the shop will be called when he takes over?
19 Why does Hobson go for his hat?
20 What does Willie finally want to buy?

Who said that, and to whom?

1 'I might find some if I looked hard.'
2 '... if you don't mend your manners I'll certify you for a lunatic asylum.'
3 'I'll have him treated with respect.'
4 'She mustn't have things too much her way.'
5 '... if I'm to come into a thing I like to know what I'm coming into.'
6 'If we come here, we come here on my terms.'
7 'You're not for me, so you're against me.'
8 'Maggie, I reckon your father could do with a bit of fresh air after this.'
9 'Words came out of my mouth that made me jump at my own boldness ...'
10 '... we'll not forget the truth about ourselves.'

Take your time questions

1 Explain in detail, in your own words, how Hobson tries to keep control of the situation in Act Four, even though he fails.
2 At the end of the play how would you sum up the characters of Alice and Vickey?
3 Look five years into the future after the end of the play and describe what you think might be the lifestyles of Hobson's three daughters.

■ How to write an examination essay

Some of you will be studying *Hobson's Choice* as one of your set texts for GCSE English Literature and will need to answer a question on it in your examination. In order to be ready for the examination, you will need to have carefully studied the plot, characters, themes and issues of the text. You will also be expected to have considered the play from a 'performance' angle. Reading this guide in an active manner will have helped you to achieve all of this, but you will also need to learn how to write an examination essay so that you do not lose marks. Study the following guidelines and then read the sample examination questions.

Answer the question asked

Many candidates lose marks because they have misread or misinterpreted the question, under pressure of time. Make sure that you know what the question requires from you and that you answer it directly, without waffling. Another common mistake happens when students have written a *similar* essay for practice *before* the exam. In trying to rewrite their old essay, they fail to notice that the exam essay is asking something slightly different. It hardly ever pays to learn essays off by heart.

Do not just retell the story

The skills required for just retelling the plot are not enough to get you a good grade at GCSE. The examiner assumes you know the story and accepts that you may have to relate a little of it to show what you mean, but this should be kept to a minimum. In an exam, you will be asked to *explore*, *examine*, *imagine*, *describe* but never to simply *retell*.

Plan your essay

You should always make time to do a short plan of your answer, however worried about time you are. Make a list of points to be included and then decide on the best order for them. It is often a good idea to check them off as you are writing, to make sure you do not miss any. Doing a plan helps you to avoid one of the most common pitfalls of examinations: failing to answer the question properly. This 'thinking' time is essential for good organisation and structure of your essay.

Starting to write

The opening few sentences can often be the most difficult to write, and can take the longest to think about. It is essential that they actually *address the question* because this will set your essay off on the right lines from the very beginning.

Quotation

You should quote in order to back up the points you are making. There is no point in quoting lengthy chunks of the text simply for the sake of it; this wins you no marks. Only quote as much as you need to prove your point.

Technical points to keep in mind

- Write your essay in formal English. Never use slang and do not write as if you were speaking.
- Organise your essay into paragraphs.
- Check your spelling. Accurate spelling is rewarded. Careless spelling mistakes create a bad impression.
- Use punctuation appropriately and correctly. Do not confuse the possessive apostrophe with plurals.
- Take care over the presentation of your essay. Write legibly and avoid crossing out too many words or sentences. Many crossings out indicate a lack of planning.

Example questions

There are several different types of question which you ought to be able to recognise.

1 First of all there are what can be called standard literary criticism type questions. These will ask you about the characters, about the text and will expect you to analyse, comment and to express a personal opinion. For instance:

   (a) 'The play is about Willie and his development into a successful business man.' Do you think this is true? (A model answer outline for this question is provided on page 54.)

   (b) 'The play is about real people leading real lives.' Choose two or three of the leading characters from the play and describe how, for you, they are 'real' people.

   (c) 'The play is about relationships between men and women.' Describe how these relationships develop through the play.

2   Another type of question can be called the text-based question. Here you will be given a short passage from the play to read and you will then be asked a question which will use this passage as its starting point. In the exam the extract will be given in full.

(a) **Maggie**   You and I'ull be straight with one another, father. I'm not a fool, and things may as well be put in their places as left untidy.

Hobson   I tell you my mind's made up. You can't have Willie Mossop. Why, lass, his father was a workhouse brat. A come-by-chance.

Maggie   It's news to me we're snobs in Salford. I'll have Willie Mossop. I've to settle my life's course, and a good course, too, so think on.

Hobson   I'd be the laughing-stock of the place if I allowed it. I won't have it, Maggie. Its hardly decent at your time of life.

Maggie   I'm thirty and I'm marrying Willie Mossop. And now I'll tell you my terms.

Hobson   You're in a nice position to state terms, my lass.

Maggie   You will pay my man, Will Mossop, the same wages as before. and as for me, I've given you the better part of twenty years of work without wages. I'll work eight hours a day in future and you will pay me fifteen shillings by the week.

Hobson   Do you think I'm made of brass?

Maggie   You'll soon be made of less than you are if you let Willie go. and if Willie goes, I go. That's what you've got to face.

Hobson   I might face it, Maggie. Shop hands are cheap.

Maggie   Cheap ones are cheap. The sort you'd have to watch all day, and you'd feel happy helping them to tie up parcels and sell laces with Tudsbury and Heeler and Minns supping their ale without you. I'm value to you, so's my man; and you can boast it at the 'Moonraker's' that your daughter Maggie's made the strangest, finest match a woman's made this fifty year. And you can put your hand in your pocket and do what I propose.

Hobson   I'll show you what I propose Maggie. (*He lifts the trap and calls.*) Will Mossop! (*He places hat on counter and unbuckles belt.*) I cannot leather you, my lass. You're female, and exempt, but I can leather him. Come up, Will Mossop.

This extract is from near the end of Act One. What do we learn about the relationship between Hobson and Maggie from this passage? What happens immediately after this exchange?

(b) Read the passage of the play from Willie's speech at the beginning of Act Three to Maggie's: 'He'll do. Another twenty years and I know which of you three men 'ull be thought most of at the Bank.' (In the exam the extract would be printed in full, as in **(a)** above.)

Describe the process of Willie's education throughout the play. What do you think of Maggie's final statement in this extract?

(c) Read the passage in Act Four, starting with Hobson's speech 'Look here, Maggie, you're talking straight and I'll talk straight and all …' through to Vickey's comment, 'Oh, but it can't be me. In my circumstances, Maggie!' (In the exam the extract would be printed in full, as in **(a)** above.)

Analyse the attitude of the three daughters.

3 A third type of question is often called the 're-creative' response. You might be asked to think about a character and to develop that character further; you might be asked to write an additional scene to the play. You are being asked to 're-create' in ways which fit in with the play.

(a) 'A typical evening at the Moonraker's'. Write an additional scene for the play where Hobson is spending an evening with his friends.

(b) Describe in detail what you think happens to Will and Maggie after they walk out of Hobson's shop, as they begin to set up their own business.

(c) Towards the end of the play Willie describes how he intends to change the shop. Write a short scene where Willie is describing his plans to Tubby. Then write a short scene, set one month later, when Alice comes to buy a new pair of boots. (A model answer outline for this question is provided on page 55.)

Model answer outlines

1 (a) This title is set in the expectation that you will agree with the statement. It would be difficult to argue that we don't see Willie developing into a successful businessman, but you could of course argue that this is not the only thing that the play is about. You could argue that the play is also about the break-up of the Hobson family, is about the demise of Hobson, and so on. Such comments could be the basis of either an opening or a closing paragraph.

- Your opening paragraph will either be a brief statement of agreement or will explore the idea suggested above.

- The central part of the essay will explore the development of the character of Willie Mossop, pointing out clearly the complete contrast between his behaviour at the beginning of the play and at the end. In terms of a successful businessman you should write about such things as the determination to turn the shop into a pleasant place for customers, the leather seats and carpets that he plans; this shows an instinctive business sense which Hobson never had.

- Your conclusion will be a brief statement describing how the character analysis has shown Willie's development, or you might choose to briefly explore other central themes of the play if you did not do so in your introduction.

 Remember to use plenty of supporting references from the text to back up your ideas. Quotation is the most direct way of giving evidence.

3 (c) In writing scenes of this type, the most important thing is to make sure that you get the characters right, and that they continue to sound like the same people. You might think of the 'Lancashire' aspects of the play, and perhaps see if you can bring some of the phrases and ideas into your writing.

You must also think carefully about the atmosphere you want to create in the scene. What is assumed here is that Tubby continues to work in the shop, and one thing that would have to be established is the changed relationship between Willie and Tubby. Tubby used to be senior to Willie, and might well be rather nervous in establishing a new relationship; hopefully Willie would be sensitive to this, and would remember that Tubby was once his teacher. Similarly, the right relationship will need to be established in the scene with Alice. She will almost certainly be overconfident when she first comes in, but she will probably not expect what she sees in the shop, and will have to adjust to the changes.

You will need to decide who will appear in your scenes. At their simplest the first scene will just be between Tubby and Willie, and the second scene between Maggie and Alice, but you might decide to bring others in. Might Maggie or Hobson be around while Willie is talking to Tubby? If Hobson is there, will he try to say anything? Might Albert come to collect Alice? Might Willie come in while Maggie is serving Alice and, if so, what would the reaction be? You need to ask yourself these questions while planning your answer.

 It is particularly important that you plan your answers to this sort of question very carefully. When you come to writing make sure that your scenes are not just a series of one line exchanges; give the characters substantial speeches

■ How to write a coursework essay

Coursework may mean preparing one piece for your coursework folder which could meet a number of requirements.

(a) It would be suitable as a submission for twentieth century drama in the English Literary Heritage.

(b) It is a very good vehicle for considering a work in its historical context.

(c) It is very suitable as a consideration of the cultural context of a piece of literature.

(d) It is equally suitable as a consideration of its social context.

In setting a coursework task, your teacher would be considering what purpose this piece of coursework should have in terms of your coursework as a whole. Sections of this book will help you in various ways, for instance:

- the historical context can be considered via the theme of family relationships and the roles played by the individual character;

- the cultural context will involve consideration of the Lancashire background of the play as well as the theme of 'industry' and the relationships between characters; and so on.

Writing the coursework essay

- It is essential that you make a plan before you begin to write. Think about the key points of the play that are relevant to your essay.

- Always do a rough draft of your coursework. Listen to the suggestions that your teacher makes after reading your rough draft and amend your draft accordingly.

- Check your best draft carefully for spelling, punctuation and grammar.

Quotation

You should quote in order to back up the points you are making. There is no point in quoting lengthy chunks of the text; this wins you no marks. Simply quote as much as you need to prove your point. Four lines at a time is probably the absolute maximum.

How long should my essay be?

This is like asking 'how long is a piece of string?' Essentially it should be as long as it needs to be to answer the question fully and well; remember that a long essay is not necessarily a good essay. What the examiner wants to see is the quality of your ideas, and this will probably be clear by the end of one or two sides of writing. You might want to write more than that to demonstrate that you can sustain and develop an idea. However, the danger in writing too much is that you might repeat yourself, which will gain you no marks. You should plan what you are going to write, and make sure that everything you say is relevant and concise. Write a second draft, and then stop. Check with your teacher for specific word limits.

Example

Let us consider a possible coursework task:

Analyse what we find out about the social background to the play and how the characters fit into that social context.

Make a list of the aspects you might want to touch on in your answer:

- the Lancashire background;
- Mrs Hepworth's social position;
- how Ada Figgins is viewed and dealt with by Maggie;
- the place of the man in the social order;
- Willie's background – his father in the workhouse; etc.

When you have your list begin to sort it, order it and to decide on your approach. You might choose to set the Hobson family firmly in the centre of your essay and look at others in relation to them. You might start at the top of the social order by writing about Mrs Hepworth, and then look at the social order of the other characters. Willie's position in the social order clearly changes from the beginning of the play to the end, whereas Tubby stays in the same place. By marrying Albert, Alice's social position changes. However you choose to deal with the topic, make sure that you remain consistent and concise.

 Remember that with coursework you have the huge advantage that you can plan and re-plan, draft and re-draft. With an examination answer you may only get one chance but there cannot be an excuse for a badly shaped piece of coursework.

Make sure that you don't leave your coursework to the last minute.

Self-test answers Act One

Uncover the plot

1 Hobson is late because he was at a meeting of the Masons the night before.
2 Albert wants to leave immediately once he finds out that Hobson is still at home and may appear at any moment.
3 It is significant because Albert is the son of a solicitor and works in the same business himself.
4 It is a meeting for a drink with his friends at the 'Moonraker's'.
5 Hobson describes a bustle as 'a hump added to nature'.
6 Tubby is the chief cobbler, and either he made the shoes himself or he will know who did make them.
7 Willie Mossop made Mrs Hepworth's shoes.
8 Mrs Hepworth gives Willie her card so that he will be able to let her know if he leaves employment with Hobson to go elsewhere.
9 Mrs Hepworth compares Willie to a rabbit.
10 She makes the comparison because he disappears down the trapdoor at speed, like a rabbit disappearing for safety into its burrow.
11 Hobson thinks that praising a workman to his face will make him 'uppish'.
12 The only evidence is that Jim Heeler says that Hobson is the best orator at the 'Moonraker's' – this does not necessarily mean that he is any good.
13 In this context 'temperance' means teetotal, that is young men who don't drink alcohol, which in the light of Hobson's own reputation is rather ironic.
14 He means that he will put his hand deep into his pocket (spend generously) to pay for the wedding (he later draws the line at paying a settlement in addition).
15 'Tokened' means that Willie is engaged to be married to Ada Figgins.
16 Maggie knows who Ada is because she brings Willie his lunch every day.
17 Willie is frightened of Mrs Figgins.
18 Maggie has decided that until they marry Willie will live at Tubby's house.
19 Maggie will protect Willie from Mrs Figgins by sending Tubby round to collect his things rather than Willie having to go himself.
20 It is an hasty and angry kiss with no passion. Willie only kisses Maggie to spite Hobson.

Who said that, and to whom?

1 Maggie says this when she is making Albert buy a pair of shoes.
2 Hobson is talking to his daughters.
3 Hobson says this to Vickey.
4 Hobson says this to Maggie.
5 Hobson says this to his daughters when he is annoyed that Mrs Hepworth has praised Willie.
6 Maggie says this to Willie.
7 Willie says this to Maggie – he doesn't understand why she wants to marry him.
8 This is Hobson telling Maggie why she can't marry Willie.
9 Willie is responding to Hobson's threat to beat him.
10 Maggie says this to Willie at the end of the Act.

Take your time questions

1 i) To draw the set, whether in plan form or as an artist's impression, means following carefully the precise instructions which are given in the long opening stage direction.

ii) Drawing or describing the costume designs requires you to do some research into the dress of the 1880s, and then to choose the right ones for the play. For instance Mrs Hepworth, Alice and Vickey may wear dresses with bustles, as these were the fashion, whereas Maggie would probably not, at least at the beginning of the play. Tubby is described as wearing a coloured shirt with no collar, but the style of the shirt will depend on what you find out about the clothes that tradesman of the period wore. Hobson's hat is carefully described in the stage direction: 'It is one of these felt hats which are half-way to tall hats in shape.' what does this mean? 'His clothes are bought to wear' means that Hobson wears serviceable, well cut clothes of the period, ordinary and not fancy.

iii) Your paragraph will almost certainly refer back to the earlier part of this answer. The set as described is very much of the period. The clothes definitely belong to the period, e.g. the dialogue about bustles. The whole ethos of the shoe shop belongs to the period in which the play is set, as do the attitudes and relationships. It is quite clearly not set in the present day.

2   Hobson does not approve of his daughters' dresses, and this provides you with a starting point for your answer.

Alice and Vickey are determined to dress fashionably, and at this time the bustle was the height of fashion. Hobson says that he likes to see his daughters looking nice, and he pays the draper to make sure that they do. He is, however, concerned if he feels that they are going too far. He draws a distinction between 'nice dressing' and 'grand dressing'. He thinks that the bustle is preposterous, and describes it as 'a hump added to nature'. Hobson regards himself as sensible and middle class, and that means that he wants his daughters to remain sensible and unpretentious. Unfortunately the girls don't see his distinction, as far as they are concerned they can either dress fashionably or they can dress like the girls who work in the mills.

Hobson makes one last attempt to convince them by drawing the distinction between a French Madam and a sensible English woman, but this doesn't work either. Both Hobson and his daughters are stubborn, and there is a complete lack of mutual understanding. There is also snobbery, particularly on the part of the girls.

3   With this question you must think carefully about Maggie's character and try to imagine what her life must be like. We know that Maggie is thirty and that she has been in charge of things since her mother died. We know from his character that Hobson expects everything to run smoothly at the shop, and we know from their characters that Maggie's sisters are not likely to be much help.

Maggie is likely to be up early every day to do the housework before it is time to open the shop. The housework will include dusting and sweeping and doing the laundry, probably in a large bowl using a washboard and a mangle. You may need to find out what these things are. Maggie will probably do the cooking, which will include preparing the breakfast and planning the meals for the rest of the day. It is likely that the rest of the family will get up later than Maggie and eat their breakfast without a thought.

Through the day Maggie is likely to spend the majority of her time in the shop, where we know she is a good salesperson. You may decide to bring several different types of people into your account.

Maggie's life is humdrum. As you continue with your account try to get the feel of her repetitive existence.

■ Self-test answers Act Two

Uncover the plot

1 Trade has gone down at Hobson's, especially the high-class trade.
2 They can make clogs to stockpile.
3 Alice finally makes the decision.
4 Alice can't add up.
5 Vickey reveals to Alice that a young man is interested in her.
6 Maggie knows where he is – asleep in Beenstock's cellar.
7 The shop is at 39a Oldfield Road, Salford.
8 Alice wants to know where the money ('the capital') has come from.
9 Maggie makes them kiss Willie.
10 They are getting married at St Philip's Church at one o'clock that day.
11 Maggie buys a brass curtain ring to use as a wedding ring.
12 Willie takes off his coat and detachable cuffs.
13 They take two fairly decrepit chairs and an old sofa.
14 They are having a 'wedding-spread' and they need somewhere for the guests to sit.
15 Albert has a document for action against Hobson for trespass.
16 Fred is to go and put the document on Hobson.
17 Albert, to his disgust, is sent with the handcart to deliver the furniture to Maggie and Willie's house.
18 Tubby is in charge.
19 Willie makes it sound as if he is going to the dentist.
20 Tubby throws old shoes after them for luck.

Who said that, and to whom?

1 Alice is telling Vickey that she can't add up.
2 Maggie is talking to her sisters.
3 Maggie is talking to Alice, saying that she always knows what she is doing.
4 Maggie is talking about her father to Alice.
5 Vickey says this when she is made to kiss Willie.
6 Alice says this to Maggie about Maggie taking the old furniture.
7 Maggie is talking to Freddie and Albert about helping to fetch the furniture.
8 Albert is talking to Maggie about pushing the handcart through the streets.
9 Maggie is talking to Willie.
10 Maggie is talking to Vickey – Maggie has the ring.

Take your time questions

1 This question requires you to think about one of the characters so that you can write about his behaviour during an incident that is important to the play, but that doesn't actually occur in the play.

As Hobson returning from the 'Moonraker's' on this particular night you are, of course, drunk. You may well be rather morose after a heavy night's drinking with Jim Heeler and your other friends. You will probably have been speaking far too much in the pub, giving your views on a whole range of topics: politics, the state of the world, and so on. You probably have to walk home alone as the others have gone off in the opposite direction. The pavement may feel uneven; occasional carts or carriages may go by; it may be raining. Suddenly there is no pavement and you feel yourself falling into a black hole. You land on something soft.

As always with this sort of question use your imagination, but don't lose touch with the facts that you know from the play, or with what you already know about the character.

2   Much of what you will write in answer to this question can be found in the section of this book that discusses Maggie's character (pages 12–14). However, write your answer before you turn back to that section. Remember to include details about:
- appearance;
- actions;
- attitude to other characters;
- attitudes of other characters to Maggie;
- opinions.

3   When writing about snobbery you are largely going to be writing about Alice, with some mention of Vickey and Hobson. Again you will need to refer to the section of this book that deals with characters (page 10).

At the beginning of the play we see that Alice regards herself highly because she is being courted by a lawyer, and the theme develops from here. What makes it impossible for snobbery to triumph is the down to earth attitude of Maggie and Willie, especially when Maggie rides rough shod over the snobbish doubts of others, for example when she makes Albert wheel the handcart through the streets of Salford.

In your answer, as well as referring to the characters, make sure that you refer to the details in the play that illustrate the different aspects of snobbery.

■ Self-test answers Act Three

Uncover the plot
1   Firstly, she thinks that they have had enough speeches, and secondly she thinks that Albert's speech would not be as good as Willie's.
2   Alice still wants to know where the money came from to set up the shop.
3   They are given the clue that the money came from the same place as the hothouse flowers.
4   Maggie tells him to clear the pots away.
5   They decide to help because until they are safely married to Alice and Vickey it is important that they keep on the right side of Maggie.
6   He wants Albert and Freddie to stay because he is nervous about being on his own with Maggie.
7   Hobson knocks at the door.
8   She sends them all into the other room, the bedroom.
9   Maggie offers him stewed tea.
10   She insists he eats it because it is her wedding cake.
11   She offers to leave because she is a woman, and normally men would discuss business in private.
12   He has come because of the writ.
13   He tries to blame Maggie for everything.
14   Hobson thinks that the *Salford Reporter* and the *Manchester Guardian* might print his story.
15   Hobson is worried by Willie's suggestion that he might lose the position of vicar's warden.

16 Albert is called out first because he is a lawyer.
17 He tries to claim one thousand pounds.
18 Maggie says that Hobson will only pay five hundred pounds.
19 The money is to provide Alice and Vickey with marriage portions.
20 'There is always room at the top', and 'Great things grow from small'.

Who said that, and to whom?

1 Alice says this to Albert to prevent him from making a speech at the wedding reception.
2 Albert is talking to Freddie when they are debating whether to help Willie with the clearing up.
3 Maggie is giving instructions to Willie before she lets Hobson in.
4 Hobson is beginning to explain to Maggie what has happened to him.
5 Willie is speaking more or less to himself, but is not cheering Hobson up.
6 Hobson is giving Albert his views on the legal profession.
7 Maggie begins to explain to Hobson that the money will be providing marriage settlements for her sisters.
8 Hobson puts on a brave face to his daughters when he knows he has lost.
9 Maggie is talking to her sisters and Albert and Freddie, expressing her confidence in the future.
10 Maggie is reading what Willie has written on his slate.

Take your time questions

1 This question asks you to give some careful consideration to the development of Willie's character during the first part of the play.

We have seen Willie initially as the frightened young worker who is scared to appear from the cellar because he believes that it will inevitably mean him being punished. He has since been taken in hand by Maggie and has begun to develop his education, his confidence and his business acumen. Mrs Hepworth, too, has had faith in Willie's abilities and helped to give him confidence in his work.

As with the preliminary character study that you have already written about Maggie, you should first think your answer through without using the character section of this book. The key to the character study is to consider what other characters think of Willie, and what he thinks of the other characters.

2 Mrs Hepworth affects the action of the play very much because she enables Maggie and Willie to develop their lives after they have left Hobson. She has not only lent them the capital, but has also provided a number of customers for the new shop.

You should look very carefully at her first appearance in Act One of the play, and should consider how she spoke to Hobson and the others. This will remind you that she is both forthright and sensible in her approach to everything, and that her compliment regarding Willie's shoemaking abilities was very significant in the development of Maggie and Willie's relationship. The provision of Maggie's wedding bouquet again shows her kindness.

It is not necessary to write a particularly long answer to this question, but it demonstrates the theme of generosity in the play.

3 i) To draw the set, whether in plan form or as an artist's impression, means following carefully the precise instructions which are given in the long opening stage direction.

ii) In order to answer this question you will have had to do some research. You may have used a costume book before that may have had some pictures of shoes in it. The very fashionable ladies' shoes at the time would have been small, tight-fitting heeled boots, probably with a lot of buttons which would have been fastened with a button hook.

iii) We have a lot of clues about the business, some of which are listed below. You will no doubt be able to think of others.

- The premises are poor, but well set out.
- Great thought is given to the comfort and convenience of the customer.
- Business cards have been printed.
- Mrs Hepworth has introduced some high-class customers
- Willie works hard and maintains the very high quality of workmanship.

■ Self-test answers Act Four

Uncover the plot

1 Lord Beaconsfield – he is also known as Benjamin Disraeli, and he was the Prime Minister.
2 He is having to do the housekeeping, including the cooking.
3 Tubby says that it is temper and obstinacy that are ruining the shop.
4 The shop assistants are men.
5 Tubby wants to go and get Maggie.
6 Hobson is afraid of committing suicide – water makes him think of drowning himself, and the razor makes him think of cutting his throat.
7 The fact that Hobson is downstairs means that he could have gone to the surgery rather than getting the doctor round to the house.
8 Jim Heeler has to leave the room.
9 The diagnosis is chronic alcoholism.
10 The doctor won't take his fee until he feels he has earned it.
11 He prescribes a female relative to keep an eye on him.
12 He wants Maggie to discipline Hobson.
13 Alice regards where she lives, the crescent, as infinitely superior.
14 Vickey is pregnant.
15 Vickey and Alice are worried that Hobson will leave all of his money to Maggie and Willie.
16 Willie speaks the way he does because he is now confident, and Maggie has told him to be 'strong'.
17 Willie finally reveals that it was Mrs Hepworth who lent them the money to set up the shop.
18 Willie insists that the shop is called 'Mossop and Hobson'.
19 Hobson needs his hat to go with Maggie to the lawyers to draw up the deed of partnership.
20 Willie wants to buy Maggie a proper wedding ring.

Who said that, and to whom?

1 Tubby is talking to Hobson about the possibility of finding work in the workshop.
2 Dr Macfarlane is talking to Hobson.
3 Maggie is talking to her sisters about Willie.
4 Vickey is talking to Alice, saying that Maggie shouldn't be allowed to inherit all of Hobson's money.

5   Willie says this to Vickey when he is up a ladder examining the stock in Hobson's shop.
6   Willie is explaining to Alice the basis on which he and Maggie might come to live with Hobson.
7   Hobson is talking to Alice and Vickey.
8   Willie is suggesting to Maggie that she should take a walk with her father to see Albert.
9   Willie is talking to Maggie.
10 Maggie is explaining to Willie why she will go on wearing the brass ring.

Take your time questions

1   Initially Hobson appears to be in control by refusing to allow Tubby to manage him in any way. He will not eat what Tubby has prepared, and he will not allow Tubby to go and find Maggie. However, his appearance immediately reveals that he is out of control.

He tries a mixture of rudeness and blustering to take control of the situation when the doctor arrives, but it is a futile effort. When he sees his daughters he tries a mixture of ordering and cajoling, believing that he will be able to get his own way with them. He finds that he has no control here either.

Similarly, and much to his surprise, he finds that he cannot exercise any control over Willie, and this perhaps finally brings him to the realisation that he is most certainly no longer in control at all.

2   When you have written your answer look back to the character descriptions of Alice and Vickey on pages 16–18. The most important thing to make clear is that Alice and Vickey are two different characters, and it is important to distinguish between them. Remember that Alice is a snob, and Vickey is in the process of becoming a doting mother.

3   This question is an invitation to use your imagination, and it is important that you do so. It is also important that you use the clues in the play to make sure that your writing fits in with what has gone before.

- Maggie has confidently predicted all along that Willie will be the most successful of the three husbands. Some things you might like to consider include:
- Will Maggie and Willie have moved into the city centre?
- Will Maggie and Willie have more than one shop?
- Vickey will have one child, possibly more – will the others have any children?
- Will Alice have become completely insufferable?